C000152349

BEFORE THERE WAS AN AFTER

Hope and Healing on Our Journey
through Addiction

Gerad Davis and Lisa Mead

ISBN: 979-8-9883988-0-6

This book is dedicated to:
All those still fighting the fight and the families that love them

And to Gerad:

Before my eyes,
you slipped away, one breath, one moment at a time.
Before my eyes,
you swam into a sea of misery, struggling, sinking to an endless
rocky bottom.
Before my eyes,
you began searching for a reason and found acceptance
and forgiveness along the way.
Before my eyes,
you surfaced and became the man you were meant to be changing
my life forever.

Lisa Mead

Contents

When your heart
is breaking for someone
who is broken, but your
words can't reach them,
ask the angels to go where
you cannot. To whisper into
their heart what their ears
can't hear: "We will not
give up on you. Don't
give up on yourself."

Sandra Kring

Author's Note

The idea for this book came during Gerad's first sustained period of sobriety. He was living in a sober house in a small town in the dead of winter. He had no vehicle and seemed restless, unsure how to navigate the world sober. I suggested he write his story to occupy his time, and perhaps he could turn it into a book. He liked the idea but wasn't sure where to start. He had mentioned that he was asked to write his life story and share it with the group during rehab, so I suggested he start with what he had already written. I gave him an iPad and a keyboard.

I would check in with him periodically and ask how the writing was going. He would express doubts about his ability to write, let alone write an entire book. I realized how little I knew about his life during those years and was certain he had no idea what we had all been through in navigating addiction, so I suggested we tell the story from each of our perspectives. Doing it together seemed less daunting to Gerad. I never saw what he wrote during that time since the iPad was one of the things eventually lost, traded, or sold for drugs. My chapters sat idle on my computer.

I brought the idea up again during the pandemic when once again, he was sober with too much time on his hand. I would write a chapter and send it to him, and he would write about the same time period from his perspective. Once he began working again and busying himself with meetings and sponsoring others in recovery, the process slowed. I assumed he was just busy, but then it dawned on me that I had never asked him if writing the book was difficult for him. I was asking him to write about the most difficult period of his life and, quite frankly, shine a light on some pretty awful things he had done and been through. His response was that yes, it was hard, but if telling his story could help just one addict, it was worth it.

The goal became not just to tell the story but to write a book that could help others who were navigating addiction. I made so many mistakes. I wish I had been able to talk to someone that had been through it with their child, but they are hard to find. The stigma of addiction creates a vacuum for those seeking any information. You are left scouring the internet for answers. We hope this book serves as a resource of hope and possibilities. You can survive this, and you will with the right information and the right support.

Preface

I smiled as I descended the stairs to my granddaughter's room, her dwarf hamster in hand. Today was her 8th birthday, and things were looking up. After a stressful two weeks, the pet store was able to find the "hamster of her dreams," as she had enthusiastically described it to me, and her dad, my son Gerad, was home, sober, and would be attending her party for the first time in four years. I had asked him to go pick up the hamster with me, but he opted to stay home so he could finish his gift to her, a beautiful series of flowers hand painted on her bedroom furniture. This would be her best birthday ever. Once Gerad had arrived at the house fresh out of detox, I had been granted a reprieve from making up another excuse as to why daddy couldn't come to her party. Things were finally getting back to normal.

As I stepped on the landing of the stairs, I could smell the trappings of art in progress, paint and turpentine, but oddly, complete silence. I assumed Gerad had taken a break and gone upstairs, but the bedroom light was on, so maybe he was just deep in concentration. I stopped in the doorway and felt a wave of warmth move up my neck and face as my heartbeat began to race. Gerad appeared to be asleep on the bed. As I looked toward the furniture he was supposed to be painting, I noticed just a few strokes of red paint. My gaze moved to the floor where a syringe with the needle still attached lay discarded.

Time slowed down and I was frozen in place. All my hopes turned into the delusions they really were, and all my denials came crashing down into the reality that my son was a hopeless heroin addict and I had failed again. I could not fix him; I could not fix this family. He was going to die.

Chapter One

The Abyss: Lisa

"He is free to evade reality,
He is free to unfocus his mind and stumble blindly
down any road he pleases, but not free to avoid the abyss
he refuses to see."
Ayn Rand

I sat in a chair next to my son's hospital bed staring out the window. I don't recall what I saw out that window; just that staring gave me something to do. There is no sense of time in hospital rooms, only the movement of people in and out to give you a sense of the passage of day into night and into the next day. Maybe the lack of that sense came from my desire to freeze time at this moment when I knew my son was safe in a cocoon where the drugs and all that went with them couldn't reach him. When someone you love is an addict, you live to get them from one safe place to another. Don't let the word safe fool you—I'm talking about hospitals, jails, detox centers, and rehabs. When Gerad was young, I did my best to prevent him from ending up in those places, but now when he was in them, I could sleep, I could eat, I could exhale.

An infection in his hand had begun to attack the bone in his thumb. Gerad had lost the feeling in his right hand because of an accident, so it was his injection site of choice for his drug of choice, heroin. Dear God…heroin…I still couldn't wrap my head around it. Two surgeries later, we still weren't sure if enough had been done

1

to save the hand. Post-operative care would be important, with high doses of antibiotics required.

Gerad didn't have a place to live. I had only been able to keep him in the hospital because they were giving him pain meds. I had been honest with the doctor about Gerad's situation, and he promised me he would keep him in the hospital for as long as he could to buy him a few days off the street. His brothers and I had been taking turns in a vigil to keep him there. I was scheduled to go on a long-planned trip in a few days. Whenever Gerad was home, I canceled all plans to keep a sobriety watch. Many trips and events fell by the wayside. It was always a struggle to know what to do. I knew whether I stayed or went, it wouldn't change things for him. As soon as his hospital stay came to an end, he'd be right back out on the street looking for his next fix. It had taken several years and several canceled trips to come to that realization.

I glanced over at my sleeping son and wondered for the millionth time if any part of the Gerad I knew was still in there. Through all the trials and tribulations of his addiction, I clung to who Gerad had been before heroin hijacked his brain. But he wasn't the same. When I told him I had to leave town, his reaction was typical and manipulative, evoking my own guilt and shame. "Go ahead and leave me; go on your vacation. You don't care about me anyway." He had become a master at tapping into my mom guilt. It didn't matter that I was taking his daughter on a Disney cruise. He couldn't see past his own misery. His brothers offered to take on the babysitting in my absence. We had all sacrificed a lot in the past few years. I got the call from his brother as our ship set sail; Gerad had snuck out of the hospital. His brother was riddled with guilt. Loving an addict is its own special kind of hell: isolating, terrifying, heartbreaking, a never-ending abyss. These were the times I wished I could stop loving him so much.

I had convinced Gerad to come to the ER that time under the threat that he could lose his hand. That was the only time I had gotten through to him in a long while, but still, he was reluctant to go.

I worked at a medical office, so I had one of our physician assistants look at his hand a few minutes before we were scheduled to close, so Gerad wouldn't have to face too many people. He told us the condition of the hand was way beyond what he could handle and called the hand surgeon, who asked us to meet him at the emergency room. I got Gerad there, but I could see his agitation rise.

He had been living in the shadows. A few weeks before, he had asked me to meet him in a Walgreens parking lot. As I circled the lot, I spotted him; his body pressed against the wall hiding from those who were coming and going. Despite the drugs numbing most of his feelings, he was ashamed of his appearance and ashamed of being a heroin addict. Coming into such a public place was uncomfortable. I was struck that he felt shame. Honestly, I thought he was beyond caring at this point. I asked him once if he cared anymore and if he wanted more. "Nobody chooses to be an addict, Mom." It broke my heart. It had been five years since his accident and three years since finding out he was addicted to heroin.

The spring of 2011 had been a good one for Gerad. He was attending the local university working on his bachelor's degree in art and had just been accepted to the Fine Arts program after submitting an extensive portfolio of his work. It was the first thing I can remember him really, really wanting. The wait had been excruciating as classmates let him know they had received their notification. Gerad was the last one informed, and he was jubilant. Photography was his area of interest, and he had put on two shows of his work as part of the program. He worked at a golf resort and had moved up to bartending from event set-ups and enjoyed the job. He lived with his girlfriend and their daughter. He had much to look forward to as spring moved into summer; however, summer had other things in mind.

By July, he had broken up with his girlfriend, his home was burglarized, and worst of all, he had crashed his motorcycle into a divider, where a small tree stopped his momentum. The tree hit him at the junction of his neck and right shoulder, breaking his jaw, cracking the helmet, and leaving him unconscious. Broken bones healed, and he escaped a serious brain injury, but the accident left him without the use of his right arm, his dominant hand, and with that, his dreams of pursuing photography as a career. He fell into a depression that he could not find his way out of or, more likely, didn't see the point of trying. He had trouble taking care of his daughter by himself. Simple tasks like giving her a bath highlighted his handicap. He couldn't find his footing and had trouble seeing the future he wanted. The accident that changed everything happened just 13 days before his 25th birthday.

There were some bright spots. He taught himself to play guitar with his left hand and began writing songs with a friend. They even tried some open mics around town. His songs expressed longing and regret, loneliness, and frustration, but they served as an outlet for him. He shifted from photography to painting, teaching himself to create with his left hand, and even toyed with going back to finish his degree. I encouraged him to keep a diary which he did on and off over the next few years. Later, when he was drifting in and out of our lives, I would find one of the diaries and begin to read it. I was never able to get through an entire page. My heart would race, and I felt like I couldn't breathe. His pain expressed in those pages was unbearable to read about. I can't imagine what it was like to live with it.

The first time Gerad was back in a hospital after the accident was to attempt to repair the nerve damage that caused the paralysis in his arm, hand, and shoulder. Right after the accident, he was diagnosed with a brachial plexus injury, for which the recommended treatment is to wait and allow the stretched nerve to heal. We had been told by the neurologist to wait a year and be re-evaluated. With nothing to do but wait, he grew more sullen and moodier. I tried to get him into therapy, but he would only attend one session and refused to go back. We fought in the car all the way there, and initially, he refused to even go into the office. I didn't know it then,

4

but he was already on the road to addiction, escaping the black hole of depression with various drugs.

As the one-year anniversary of his accident approached, I decided to get the process started early since Gerad soon wouldn't be covered by our insurance. I asked one of the spine surgeons in the group I worked for if he could order the MRI required by the neurologist. He examined Gerad, ordered the MRI, and advised us to go to the University of California at Davis for a second opinion. He suspected that Gerad had been misdiagnosed. The doctor wanted Gerad to see Dr. Robert Szabo, an orthopedic surgeon and professor who specialized in these types of injuries. We took his advice, and with the help of another physician, by coincidence a close friend of Dr. Szabo's, got him an appointment two days later. We felt anxious on the trip to Sacramento. I had never been to UC Davis, only driven by the medical complex on my way somewhere else. The building that housed the orthopedic department was modern, clean, and massive. Considering its size, we encountered very few people. I soon found out why; Dr. Szabo was coming in on his day off as a favor and had to see us early before the other physicians started their clinics. It felt serendipitous. All the ducks had lined up in a row.

Dr. Bray had warned me that Dr. Szabo had a very direct manner, and the residents that worked under him were apparently terrified of his wrath. After we were escorted to an exam room, a resident came in to do the initial evaluation. He was soft-spoken and efficient as he took Gerad's history. His demeanor changed immediately when Dr. Szabo entered the room. I smiled slightly at his reaction. Dr. Szabo looked at the MRI, did a quick exam, and said, "This is not a brachial plexus injury. This is a nerve root avulsion. He should have had surgery within three months of his accident." A nerve root avulsion means the nerve was pulled out of the spinal cord, unlike a brachial plexus injury which can resolve itself over time since the nerve is stretched, not avulsed. With a nerve root avulsion, the sooner the surgery is done, the better the chance of success. We were nearing the one-year mark and weren't sure if we had already missed that window. Tears welled up in Gerad's eyes and I swallowed hard.

"What do you recommend?" I asked.

"Surgery."

He explained that he only did a few of these types of surgeries a year, but there were two places in the country that did it regularly. As chance would have it, one of his former Fellows was at Mayo Clinic, and the team he had assembled did more of these repairs than anyone in the country. He asked if we would be willing to go to Rochester, Minnesota. Without consulting Gerad, I said absolutely. He told us that the evaluation to determine if the patient was a good candidate for surgery usually took a month. He would call Mayo Clinic directly and ask for the favor of getting it done in a matter of days. We were fortunate to have insurance with coverage nationwide. Despite his reputation, Dr. Szabo was clear, concise, organized, and, as we would find out, always followed through.

I felt hopeful as I left the office, but when I looked back, Gerad was bent slightly over and crying. The news had hit him hard, and what small hope had been building as we approached the one-year anniversary of his accident had vanished. We walked to the car and he slid into the backseat. For the first time, I asked him what he wanted to do. He said he didn't know. I told him I thought the surgery sounded like his only chance to regain the use of his arm and shoulder. I said that I knew it was a setback to find out he had been misdiagnosed but also how lucky I felt we were to have ended up at a place that finally got it right, just months before it was too late. He agreed to go forward. Miraculously, within 15 minutes of leaving the office, I got a call from Mayo on my cell phone. Because time was not on our side, they agreed to do a full day of appointments to have him evaluated and do surgery the next day. It was a logistical feat. We were on our way to Minnesota less than a week later.

I was as impressed with Mayo Clinic as any place I had ever been, but even more so since my entire career had been in healthcare. The buildings were more works of art than utilitarian and clinical. If you appeared to be looking for something, anyone close by would warmly ask if you need assistance. There was a piano for anyone to play, an office to deal with international patients, and a display on the history of the Mayo brothers with the motto still prominently displayed today: "The needs of the patient come first." It showed everywhere you went. Gerad was equally impressed but for different reasons. The Gondola Building is a treasure trove of original art donated by grateful patients. We walked the halls in awe and stopped and stared at an original Warhol. Dale Chihuly glass adorned one of the ceilings, and there was a giant mandala in the patient educational center with a sign requesting that patients contribute to the massive coloring project. Gerad did a small part. We asked someone about all the art, and they told us that no one had ever cataloged the artwork. I suggested to Gerad that it would be an incredible opportunity for an internship and maybe credits toward his degree. I was always trying to get him to look to a brighter future, but I was still unable to understand the depths of his depression.

The clinical process was equally impressive. We had received a schedule of appointments prior to arrival, and each went off without a hitch; nerve conduction studies, neurology, orthopedics, pain management, and neurosurgery. He would have three nerve re-implantations where nerves in his arm and shoulder that were functioning would be split and attached to the muscles where the nerves were no longer functioning. A team of orthopedists and neurosurgeons would be working with a microscope to magnify nerves the size of a thread. It seemed like a miracle. What we didn't know was that it was the beginning of the end of life as we knew it.

The conversation I remember best at the Mayo Clinic is with the pain management physician. At first, I was impressed at how efficient the process was as he explained what kind of pain to expect and handed us prescriptions to be filled at the onsite pharmacy prior to leaving. I remember the lady's infectious smile at the pharmacy's front desk. She said she loved my haircut and asked if she could take a picture of it. These were truly the nicest, most caring staff I had ever encountered in any healthcare setting. They lived the Mayo values, so as the pain doctor explained that nerve pain needed special attention and a certain mix of painkillers, I felt he had this value in mind. When he handed me the prescriptions, I mentioned that this was a lot of painkillers and asked who would monitor their use when we went home. They had given him Oxycontin, Neurontin, and Hydrocodone. He looked at me and said, "I don't think you understand how painful nerve pain can be. He will wake up in the middle of the night with searing, burning pain without the medications." We hadn't come this far to back out now. Back then, there was no assessment to determine if he was having issues with depression or if he was using drugs recreationally. Their focus was relieving his pain from this surgery. Little did any of us realize that Gerad had been easing his pain with various drugs since the accident and that the physical pain he was about to face would be the easy part.

We arrived at the hospital very early the next morning. As we walked to the reception area, we were greeted warmly by name as if we were their only patient that day. I was taken aback, and it helped set my mind at ease. It didn't seem to have the same effect on Gerad. He remained quiet and pensive, going through the motions, complying with whatever they asked him to do as he prepared for surgery. I was escorted to a waiting area with a digital board from which you could track the surgical process from pre-op to the operating room to PACU. Once Gerad entered the PACU, I was escorted to his hospital room to await his arrival. The surgery went very well, according to the doctor. Gerad would spend two nights in the hospital and, on the doctor's recommendation, spend one night upon discharge in a hotel in Rochester to make sure there were no complications. Gerad's arm was in a large, awkward splint and sling upon discharge from the hospital, but we managed to get his prescriptions and make it to the hotel to settle in. It was a very long night. Gerad was restless and didn't seem to be able to get comfortable, but we made it through and to the airport the next day. I did my best to get him settled on the plane for the trip back home. It happened to be Memorial Day weekend, and I had convinced Gerad to spend the first night home with me since he was in a large brace and still wrapped in surgical gauze and bandages. Gerad's daughter came over to see him and spend the night too. Ironically, within hours of our return, she tripped in our backyard and broke her arm. Memorial Day weekend is not an ideal time to go to the ER, so I called the orthopedist on call and asked if it could wait until Tuesday. He told me to fashion a sling and give her Tylenol. I now had two patients.

Gerad's first follow-up appointment had been scheduled by Mayo Clinic with a doctor in the group I worked for that, as luck would have it, studied under Gerad's surgeon at Mayo. The coincidences in this whole process were remarkable. It felt like it couldn't have gone any better. His daughter had her appointment with the orthopedist on the same day. Gerad would have the surgical splint removed and move into a cast. They decided to get a matching pair. She picked a purple cast with an added dose of glitter. Without hesitation, Gerad agreed. My sister-in-law happened to be taking photos at our office, so she snapped several of the casting process with them. In one, that two-year-old angel put her hand on Gerad's leg to comfort him when he cried out as they moved his arm. It is still my favorite photo of them.

During the appointment, the doctor said Gerad was healing as expected, even though he was having breakthrough pain. He had stopped the Neurontin as it had debilitating side effects, so they suggested he increase one of the other pain meds at night. He would wear the cast for six more weeks and then come back to have it removed. Once his cast was removed, they would retest his reflexes. Although they told us there had been significant trauma to his nerves with the surgery, which would take a while to heal, we had hoped for movement in his hand or arm when the cast was removed; but when the day came, nothing happened. They tested his nerve conduction with electrical stimulation but found no change. His arm hung limply by his side, the palm facing out. The only change was new scars along his arm from the surgery. We both felt defeated, but the doctor reassured us that we had to give it more time. Skeptical, we looked at each other. We had heard that before.

A few months later, we went back to Mayo for our first follow-up with Dr. Shin. We had the same series of appointments we had done at the initial evaluation, starting with neurology. After running the same nerve conduction testing that had been done in Reno after his cast was removed, the neurologist told us he detected activity in the nerves. We asked why Gerad still couldn't move his arm. Again, we were told it would take time. The orthopedic department was next. We were escorted into an exam room and when Dr. Shin arrived told him we were disappointed Gerad hadn't made any progress. He explained that because he had surgically reimplanted nerves from other muscles, Gerad had to activate the nerves differently than he had before the accident. He instructed Gerad to bend his wrist back which would activate the nerve that controlled his bicep. With a simple flick of his wrist, the bicep engaged. That was the first genuine smile and even laugh I had heard from Gerad in a long time. We were both amazed. Still on cloud nine, we were sent to hand therapy to go over the exercises Gerad would need to do to continue to make progress. We ended with a visit to the pain doctor. He handed us refills for different pain meds to take as needed, letting us know that now that Gerad would be doing therapy, his nerves would begin to "wake up" and continue the medication.

There are plenty of "what if's" in what happened. I can't blame the pain doctors at Mayo Clinic, but if he had been drug tested prior to receiving the prescriptions or tested for depression, would they have done things differently? At the time, the addictive qualities of Oxycontin were still being denied by Purdue Pharma. Should I have been more aware of the extent that Gerad was unable to cope with his post-accident life? There were hints. He received Robaxin, a liquid narcotic, upon leaving the hospital after his accident because his jaw was wired shut. He told me that after one sip, he thought, "If only I could feel like this all the time..."

I knew he was depressed, but I thought he would come around. I was now on the periphery of his life and can't remember when that line was crossed. I knew my child, but not the grown man. Everything I knew about him was based on being his mom. He told me what was suitable for my role but no longer reached out when he was hurting. He had others for that now, just as I did when I grew up and moved away. Although I understood my mother knew little of my experiences or troubles as an adult, I somehow missed when it changed with my own children. Gerad had never been in trouble, earned an associate degree, worked and paid his own bills, and was working on his bachelor's degree. He had many friends and had been in a long-term loving relationship, was an attentive father to his daughter, and was an integral part of our family and its celebrations. I saw what he wanted me to see.

We took someone that was depressed and self-medicating and gave him access to the consistent, prescribed, daily use of opioids over months and months. When the prescriptions ran out, he began to buy or steal pills from friends and family. Once he was introduced to heroin, all bets were off. He stopped answering his phone, his friends changed, and he couldn't go anywhere without nodding off. It would take me a year before I realized what was going on. One year. How did I not know? When I asked him why he didn't ask for help as things spiraled out of control, he told me he was too embarrassed. He had survived a motorcycle accident and depression and had experienced what was as close to a miracle as I had ever seen at the Mayo Clinic to end up with the worst possible outcome. I thanked God he was still alive and naively thought this could be fixed too with a lot of love and determination, except he wasn't my little boy anymore. I had no idea of the battle before us, nor did I realize how long it would take to get him back. We had fallen down the rabbit hole, and the mad queen was in control of us all.

Chapter One

The Abyss: Gerad

"If you stare into the abyss long enough,
The abyss stares back at you."
Friedrich Nietzsche

Laying in that hospital bed, all I could think was, I wish everyone would leave me alone long enough so I could get out of there. The fear of losing my hand quickly dissipated. The pain meds they gave me weren't strong enough to keep my cravings at bay, and I desperately wanted to get high enough not to feel. I spent most of my time faking sleep. I felt oddly lonely even though I was never alone. Various family members took turns watching over me, giving me little to no chance of contacting someone to rescue me. I felt anxious and sad, feelings I had been running away from since my accident. I had fallen into an abyss and saw no way out.

Depression is hard to identify when you're in the depths of it. Within a few months of my accident, I rarely left the house or showed interest in the things I used to enjoy. My mom would often come to check on me, encouraging me to get out.

"Gerad, you're depressed," she'd say as if it was the most obvious thing in the world.

"I am?" I responded. It hadn't really occurred to me.

"You need a change of scenery. Get out of the house."

Life had taken quite a drastic turn in the summer of 2011. I went from everything falling into place to being shattered into a million pieces. I was unable to process the painful events that took place, and within a few short weeks, I was losing the will to live. It felt like my life had been run through a blender, and I couldn't tell which way was up anymore. It was the first time I had ever considered ending my life. I came to believe that drugs could play a role in saving what was left and possibly open up my creative side again. Since my jaw was wired shut from the motorcycle accident, they sent me home with a bottle of liquid Roxicodone. It's hard to describe the amount of relief that just one sip of this high-powered opiate elixir offered. All the emotional and physical pain I felt was washed away in a few short seconds. I didn't realize that it would also wash away everything I loved.

I remember thinking, "If I had enough of this to last me for the rest of my life, I would be okay," so I worked to replicate that feeling with other drugs. And it worked, at least for a while. All the pain and misery that had been building up for months like a dammed river was broken as I began to produce art and music. A constant stream of work began to pour out from the depths of my soul. I learned to paint and play the guitar with my left hand and began to consider that I could pull myself out of this dark place. Creativity had always played an important role in my life, and now I believed it could get me through the most painful situation I had ever experienced. Drugs have a way of making you believe the impossible and the improbable, at least at first. I had underestimated how much of what I felt was not from my healing but from the numbing power of the drugs.

I wasn't paying attention to how many drugs I started to consume. I believed they were helping me create, so it was the least of my worries, yet the following months were still full of despair. I withdrew from the outside world because I didn't know how to sort out the new me. Although the rest of my body had healed, my right arm was still completely lifeless. It was like having a 1000-pound weight attached to my body that kept me anchored inside and out. When I was selling weed, I had tons of "friends" that were always around my house. These so-called friends vanished as soon as I lost everything. There were a select few that helped me stay afloat, and I will never forget those people for their kindness.

The loneliness consumed me; the silence was haunting. The opiates and cocaine made me numb, and that was the only thing I wanted—to block it all out. I still have mixed feelings about this time because on one side I was painting and writing songs endlessly, but on the other I was feeling myself drift into a black hole, and I didn't give a damn. I can see the selfishness in my actions now, but at the time, I felt wronged, which gave me the license to treat people however I wanted. The self-pity created this force field between me and the world. No one could question my actions because I would throw it back in their face, saying, "You would act this way too if it happened to you."

The doctors initially told me this was a temporary injury, but as far as I could tell, it wasn't getting any better. I went to so many doctors, and each time I would lose more and more hope of ever regaining control of my arm or my life. Mom organized all these appointments, but my attitude was never hopeful. When we went to the University of California at Davis to get a second opinion, and I heard for the first time what my true diagnosis was, I was so fucking angry at the doctors, at my mom, and myself. I was sitting in an all-white exam room with all these nice people with fully functioning bodies, and all I could think was, "I will never have my life back." I was sick to my stomach. Mom was trying to convince me to give this Mayo Clinic thing a shot, and I just didn't have the strength to argue. Maybe this surgery would provide some sort of normalcy. I was doing pills on a regular basis at that time, and I was worried about how I was going to keep myself "well" during this trip. While my mom was busy figuring out how to pull this off in such a short time frame, I was only worried about how to bring enough pills with me to make the trip. I brought a few with me, and I was praying that they would give me some pain medication when I got there. My mom let me drive to Rochester from the airport, and I remember feeling the heavy eyes and the nod come on. I am grateful that we made it there in one piece. This was my life now, pretending that everything was Okay when really, I was on the edge of causing irreversible damage.

The Mayo Clinic was something out of a fairytale. I couldn't believe it was an actual hospital campus. They had world-class art exhibits down every corridor. Mom and I spent the whole first day going to appointments and wandering around the beautiful land- scape. It had a way of distracting you from the medical demons that people were there to fight. It was the first time I had a glimpse of hope, and that was a far cry from the mental state I felt trapped in for the prior year. Everything moved so fast that I didn't have a mo- ment to consider what I was signing up for. Before I knew it, I was heading into surgery. Maybe this would change everything.

Mom wiped tears from my face as I woke up in a hospital room yet again. It felt like I was in a car wreck from all the different ways they bent my arm to operate on it. Nerve pain is by far the worst pain I have ever experienced. My whole right arm felt like it was burning from the inside out like they pumped my veins full of lava. All the nurses and doctors' faces blended together, my internal battle muting the external world. It was hard to pay attention to anything going on. They had me on a morphine drip, and I kept thinking, "Man, I wish I could empty that whole thing into my body right now." They had it on a timer, so I could only push the button when the machine allowed me. I watched the seconds tick by and couldn't wait for the next bit of relief. I spent a couple of days in the hospital and was released under my mom's care for one night in a nearby hotel. The first night in the hotel, I remember her waking up to check on me every time I made a grunt or shifted my body. I wondered to myself how much sleep my mom had lost since my motorcycle accident. She was a true caregiver, and I couldn't doubt how much she loved me in those moments.

The doctor sent me home with several pain medications, and I was excited because they gave me oxycodone without the acet- aminophen. This means that it makes it much easier to snort. I was eagerly waiting for the moment when my mom wasn't hovering over me. As soon as she had to go to the bathroom, I would scramble to get up, crush a couple of pills and quickly snort them before she got back. This was quite the feat considering I could barely move. My whole body felt like it was whiplashed, but the physical setback was no match for the euphoric relief. I was deceitful from the beginning because I didn't want anyone to know what my true nature had become. All I wanted was enough painkillers to keep me numb and everyone to leave me alone.

We made it back to Reno, and I was hopeful that our trip wasn't wasted. The only person I worried about was me, and then my daughter fell and broke her arm the day we got back. God has peculiar timing. It shook me out of my self-pity, at least for a while. Tatum and I both had appointments at the same time to get casts put on, and I can vividly remember her comforting me with those big blue eyes, "It's okay, daddy," while I winced in pain. She had no idea how destroyed I was on every level, but for a split second, I felt our connection, and I believed her that everything was okay.

I got my cast off several weeks later and anxiously waited for them to test my nerve function. I had learned to expect the worst at this point, yet I was especially crushed that there wasn't any activity. This was the moment that broke me. This was the moment when I declared this life pointless. It was a rollercoaster, and I was exhausted from being on that ride too long. My depression deepened.

We went back to the Mayo Clinic in December 2012 for a checkup. My arm still hung lifeless, but the nerve testing there showed activity. The surgeon asked if I had been able to move it. When I said no, he told me my nerves had been rewired, and I had to activate them differently. He showed me how to engage my bicep by lifting my wrist, and I was floored! I instantly burst into tears and was elated that I could partially move my arm. A miracle. I thought that moment would be enough for me to move forward and not want to escape, but it wasn't. It felt good not to feel, and if I had it my way, I would never feel again.

Chapter Two

Crossroads: Lisa

"There must be a few times in life
When you stand at a precipice of a decision.
When you know there will forever be
a Before and an After."
Justina Chen Headley

We all wonder if there is anything we could have done to stop someone we love from going over the edge. It's not one thing but a series of things, big and small, a hundred different choices in random order. There wasn't one crossroad but many. We can't recreate the moments, nor the order they happened in, that led to this point, and even if you could, what would it change? Still, we try, going over it repeatedly in our heads. I wanted to blame something for Gerad's susceptibility to addiction. I looked at the medical possibilities: seizures at nine months old, a head injury at four, his motorcycle accident, and head injury number two. As a young boy, he had an auditory processing disorder, which meant his brain couldn't properly translate the meaning of noises. Loud noises were frightening. That meant no parades or fireworks. Maybe it made him more sensitive to stimuli? Genetics? There were several generations of alcoholism on his dad's side. Personality? He was different than his brothers, more sensitive, and less interested in team sports or GI Joes. He was musical and artistic. He was fascinated by Rube Goldberg machines, skateboarding, and fire spinning. He liked sports cars and had his heart set on a Toyota MR2. He liked anything with wheels and going fast, with the patience and focus that gave him the ability to fix just about anything. He had golden blonde hair and blue eyes and was the most athletic of my boys, with no real interest in team sports. He was sweet, gentle, and kind. When he was young, he sat in the backseat of the car after I picked him up from a friend's house and said, "Mom, I'm not good at anything." I told him he was better at making friends than anyone I knew. That seemed to satisfy him, and he went on to make many, many friends. He always had a wide circle of them around him, and he was the ringmaster. He soon became known to them as G.

As he grew up, Gerad was easygoing but guarded, hard to read, but with a wonderful sense of humor. He didn't push our buttons but instead tried to lay low, always complying with what he was asked to do. His father and I didn't see eye-to-eye on raising children. He believed in fear as a motivator and in raising his kids to be just like him. It was hard for him to recognize how different Gerad was from his ideal. Still, they got along, Gerad learning not to rile him. I had always felt safe and loved by my father and wanted my kids to feel the same. On the rare occasion when Gerad got into trouble, he would stand in front of his father, head down, with no eye contact, and never talk back. I remember one time witnessing this and thinking he just wanted to disappear. He hated conflict. I can't remember a time when he lost his temper, no matter how hard he was pushed. He observed things keenly but didn't contribute or join in. He felt most at ease around his friends and was talkative, animated, and full of life. There were some insecurities and self-doubt, but also diligence and persistence when something piqued his interest.

Gerad's older brother Ryan once got a Power Rangers skateboard. We had just moved to Montana and were renting a house with a walkway to the front porch that was at just the right slope to keep you moving without going so fast you lost control. Ryan took the skateboard and rolled down that sidewalk, always stepping off halfway down. Gerad watched intently from the porch. Ryan soon grew tired of trying and left the skateboard in the front yard. Gerad didn't grab it, he wouldn't have risked making Ryan mad, but as soon as we moved to our new house a few weeks later, the skateboard lay forgotten in the garage. Gerad grabbed a helmet and started practicing on our driveway. He didn't stop until he conquered it. He was six years old and spent eight hours working at it until he could cruise the entire length of the sidewalk in front of our house. My dad was visiting and would come out on the porch to watch as Gerad tried, fell, and tried again. I had lost track of how long he was out there, but my dad kept coming in and reporting on his progress. When he had finally mastered it, I happened to walk outside. My dad asked if I would take a picture of him and Gerad, skateboard in hand. He put his arm around Gerad's shoulders and hugged him tightly. He looked at me and said, "Gerad never gave up!" Both were beaming. I love that picture and often think about what my dad saw that day. I clung to it in the hardest times, believing that Gerad wouldn't ever give up, and if he could keep fighting, so could I.

Like many middle children, he didn't raise any alarms and didn't get into trouble when he was young. He didn't entertain himself as well as his older brother. I remember laughing when he would come to me and say, "I'm bored," five minutes after his friend left, but he was easily redirected. He believed in adventure, and I could send him out to dig a path in the snow to his trampoline in the dead of winter or build a snow cave in the front yard. He liked to have something interesting to do. Maybe it was boredom, or perhaps he felt overlooked.

Being a "good child" often means less attention. I had an older sister that was gregarious and mischievous, and she garnered much of my parents' attention, although not in the way she wanted, and a younger brother who was the first boy in our extended family. I wasn't the prettiest or the funniest, but I was the best behaved. I was a bit of a ghost in my family, moving about rarely seen and never heard. Why didn't I pay more attention to what was happening to Gerad, knowing what it was like to slip through the cracks?

By all accounts, our happiest times were when we lived in Montana. Gerad thrived. I took the kids on hikes every weekend the weather allowed. He skied, fished, and loved starting campfires, school, and his friends. We felt stable after moving several times for my ex-husband's job and would have lived there forever. By the time Gerad was finishing elementary school, we had moved again to Nevada. I now realize just how unhappy I was in my marriage, starting over again and with a demanding job. Gerad didn't cry out for attention. I checked all the boxes for school supplies, meals, and dentist appointments, but I was going through the motions. I don't remember laughing and rarely smiled. It was only a few years, but they were critical years for Gerad. My mom overheard him explaining to a friend why she lived with us, "My dad's gone a lot, and my mom has to work all the time." His friends became his family, the people he felt he could count on. He should have been able to count on me.

If the root cause was too complicated to figure out, surely I should have seen the more obvious signs. I examined what I could have done differently. Did I know my son as well as I thought I did? Gerad was a lot like me in many ways. I wondered if he had felt the same growing up; a bit out of place, a bit scared, an observer trying to figure out how it all worked. I knew, like me, he didn't stand up for himself and had trouble saying no, which had its positives and negatives. Your friends see you as the person they can always count on to pick them up when they get stranded or give them a place to crash when they have nowhere else to go. But those same friends stay too long, don't pay rent, and never seem to be around when you need a helping hand, not that we'd ever ask. Internally resentment grows, but you still don't speak up. Peer pressure may have started him down the path of experimenting with drugs, but heroin? His life had changed dramatically since the accident. Was he trying to escape, forget, or numb the pain? I felt I hadn't given him the tools to push through, to face this challenge head-on. I had those abilities and saw the world through that lens; you never give up, but you don't get to choose the traits your children inherit. But did I inherit it, or did my parents teach it? We all have different strengths, and I wasted a lot of time pushing Gerad to get through it my way. I wish I had listened more and asked more questions, especially when things seemed off. It seems silly now, but I didn't want to be too invasive, butting into my kids' lives, especially as they got older.

Parenthood doesn't give you the insight to know everything you should about your child. Sometimes you only see what they want you to see, or worse, you only see what you want to see. I always gave my kids the benefit of the doubt and defended them fiercely. I believed I had taught them compassion, empathy, thoughtfulness, and kindness. I am sure they knew I believed in them and was their biggest supporter. That can work against you when your child becomes an addict. They use your guilt as a weapon to manipulate you. Everything you know about being a "good" parent is often the opposite of what you need to do. Even providing shelter, food, or money can prolong what you are trying to stop. You assume they are still the person you knew before the addiction, and it takes a string of disappointments to show you otherwise. These aren't their childhood disappointments, not making the team or losing their first love. This is them stealing from you and your mother, getting arrested, and choosing heroin over their own child. It is heartbreaking when you realize you can no longer trust them. They have been reduced to a petty thief, a liar, a manipulator, and someone who would do whatever it takes to get the drugs. Yet the magnet that connects a parent and child keeps pulling you back in. You finally convince yourself that it's the drug, not the child, and he is still in there underneath the haze of the drugs. So, you tell yourself you can't let him live on the street, go hungry, or go without a car or a phone. We are often too close to be able to see the truth. I always believed you had to look at the whole person, not focus on their flaws, but you can never imagine what addiction will do to them, and you need a new set of rules to survive it.

In the beginning, I truly believed we would deal with this and move on. I took control, brought him to my house, and forced him into detoxing cold turkey. I was so angry that I didn't stop to think about how to go about it. He was doing something that could kill him and had to stop. Naively I assumed he wanted to fix it too, that he would give it his all and beat this thing. That first night I told him he had to stop and get his life back, and if he didn't, he would die. "You have to fight Gerad." He looked at me slowly and deliberately through glassy eyes and the haze of the end of his high and asked, "Why?" I showed him a picture of his daughter and said, "That's why," but I still walked away shaking. I had no idea how over my head I was or how long this journey would be, but I did know there had been a seismic shift in our lives, and none of us would ever be the same.

His first detox was excruciating to watch; vomiting, diarrhea, leg cramps, cold sweats, and pain, it seemed, everywhere. Later I heard the term dope sick for the first time. It doesn't begin to describe what I was watching Gerad go through. A small part of me began to understand why it was to be avoided at all costs, even if it meant losing everything. I stayed home from work to watch him and had him sleep on the couch so I could check on him. Less than 24 hours into it, he texted a friend to get him Suboxone. I hadn't thought of taking his phone away, and I didn't even know what Suboxone was, let alone that it was sold on the street. I found out because I saw an unfamiliar car at the end of our driveway and asked Gerad what was going on. I grabbed his phone and saw the text. I texted back and told him he would go away if he cared about Gerad. The friend texted back and begged me to get Gerad something to get through the withdrawals. I didn't answer and took the phone with me, but self-doubt began to creep in. Could withdrawal kill him? Would he get desperate and leave? Like everything else in life, I stubbornly decided to stay the course.

I googled Suboxone. My initial reaction was it was trading one drug for another, but I went ahead and looked up who in the area prescribed it. When I checked on Gerad, he was rolled up in a ball on the bed. My heart broke for him. He was trying to gut it out, but I had to give him some hope of relief. I told him I found a psychiatrist that would prescribe Suboxone, but he would have to go in for regular appointments. I think Gerad would have agreed to anything at that point. By this time, Gerad had aged out of our insurance coverage, which is always the first question you get asked when seeking help for addiction. I made the call and told them I would pay cash. After I explained the circumstances, we got an appointment later that afternoon. I went back to the casita and told him he just had to hang on for a few more hours. There was no way to know that this would be attempt number one of seven to get clean.

We arrived at the office in a large historic house on a tree-lined street near downtown. I chose this psychiatrist over the other three listed because I recognized his name from my time working at the local University. I didn't know where to start on getting a recommendation for addiction treatment. I didn't know anyone that had gone through it, or at least I didn't think I knew anyone. No one talks about it. It's the great tragedy within this tragedy; you fly blind into the unknown, testing the waters. I was brimming with hope; Gerad was just trying to get relief.

The waiting area was sparse and sterile, not at all representative of the exterior's grandeur. A receptionist greeted us, and we waited in chairs that had seen better days. It was eerily quiet. Gerad looked anxious and sick. Like a bad movie, I could hear the clock ticking on the wall. The wait was lonely. I had no words of comfort to give him or myself, so we sat apart, silent. The appointment didn't take long, with questions that seemed obligatory to justify the prescription. The doctor spent most of the time explaining a book he wanted Gerad to read on research he was conducting on brain waves. He seemed somewhat detached from what Gerad was going through and disinterested. Still, we got what we came for, a prescription for Suboxone. Rx in hand, we headed to the pharmacy.

There are moments of judgment and rejection on this journey, but also amazing compassion and empathy. The last place I expected to get the former was from family and friends, and the last place I expected to get the latter was from a pharmacist at Safeway. I was too busy trying to fix the situation to stop and think about how people would react as I handed over the prescription. Suboxone is taken to suppress the withdrawal symptoms associated with opioid use. The pharmacy technician's smile disappeared when she looked at it, and she walked over to hand it to a pharmacist working on his computer. For a moment, I thought they would refuse to fill it, and I could feel the bile begin to rise from my stomach. His reaction, however, was quite different. He walked over to the window and smiled, asking if we had insurance. I told him Gerad wasn't covered, and he let us know Suboxone was quite expensive. He told us he thought he had seen a discount on the company's website that would cut the price down and walked back over to his computer. I realized I had been holding my breath and let out a sigh of relief. I watched him, brows furrowed, tapping the keyboard and staring at his screen. He was at it so long I assumed he had no luck, but as he walked back over, he held not one but three coupons which saved us hundreds of dollars. He said he had found several places that offered a discount, explained to us how the drug should be taken, and as I turned to walk away, he said, "Good luck, I'm rooting for him." I wanted to cry.

The first two weeks on Suboxone were amazing. Gerad's withdrawal symptoms went away, and his emotions returned. Later, I could always tell when he was using as his entire personality became muted; he never laughed or smiled. As he chuckled at a comment I made about his sugar cravings, I realized I hadn't seen him smile or laugh for six months. When he was clean, Gerad would let his guard down, and, in a strange way, I got to know him better. We watched the entire first and second seasons of *Game of Thrones* and talked about what he wanted to do in the future. His daughter came to visit, and naively, I tried to make life as normal as possible. By week three, I was feeling confident.

One night Gerad said he was reconnecting with old friends and had gone out to dinner. I walked over to the casita to turn off the lights he had left on and stopped in my tracks when I saw a spoon and lighter on the bathroom sink. I remember thinking how incredibly brazen to leave it out. I also felt like an idiot for asking people, "Have you seen my spoons?" for the last two weeks. I called him and asked him to come home immediately. He walked in the door as I sat on a bar stool at our island. I calmly told him what I had found and asked if he was using. He put his head down, and I knew he had. I asked what had happened to the Suboxone. He admitted he had been selling it. This was my first lesson in what life would become like in his multiple attempts to get clean: never believe what they tell you, never leave them with a phone, never leave them alone, and certainly don't be stupid enough to leave them with an entire prescription of Suboxone.

I told him he couldn't stay at the house if he was using. Somehow, I thought he would stop so he could stay. Sometimes I miss those kinds of simplistic thoughts I was capable of before all this happened. He turned and went back to the casita. A few hours later, I went to check on him and he was gone, along with a backpack with his phone, car keys, toiletries, and clothes. I panicked. I thought I had to rescue him from his own terrible decision. I called a friend that had a buddy in Search and Rescue. He suggested I talk to him. It is laughable now. Were they really going to go out and look for an addict? He kindly suggested I call the Sheriff's department and report him missing. I can't say enough about how kind the Washoe County Sheriff's Office deputies were when they showed up at my house. Can you imagine what was going through their heads? They never showed frustration and patiently asked questions. They asked for a description of Gerad and a description of his car. They told me since he was an adult, there wasn't much they could do, but they promised to look out for his car and would call me if they spotted it. I understood so little about the mind of an addict that my fear was he would try to harm himself—as if sticking a needle in your arm and injecting heroin wasn't harmful enough. The call never came from Gerad or the Sheriff's office, and so began the roller coaster of his drifting in and out of our lives, occasional sightings around town, late-night phone calls, and sleepless nights.

Chapter Two

Crossroads: Gerad

"Identity was partly heritage, partly upbringing,
but mostly the choices you make in life."
Patricia Briggs

I looked at the past, constantly wondering if I could piece together where things started to go wrong. The answer is, I don't know. I combed through my life in detail every time I got sober to try and make sense of my demise. My childhood was normal, all things considered. I never went hungry and always had a roof over my head. So, what could it be? I was different from my dad and brothers, and as I got older, I isolated myself further and further because I couldn't find common ground. My dad terrified me at times growing up, and it ultimately pushed me out the door to find something more peaceful. He would come home drunk and wake my older brother and me up to clean up whatever we had forgotten from the afternoon's activities. One night, he woke me up to go out into the backyard and pick up my toy golf clubs. Now, this wouldn't be a big deal, but we lived in Montana at the time, and as I looked out the window, I realized the ground was covered with snow. I could hardly see anything in those conditions. He threatened to send me out there with no shoes on in the middle of the night. I was around eight years old and didn't know how to process the danger I felt around him more and more. I don't believe my dad was a bad guy, but his actions fractured my trust in him; things like pouring beer in my mouth in front of a party full of people. I wore retainers grow-ing up and had a bad habit of losing them. They were expensive. My parents decided to put a permanent retainer in my mouth, so I couldn't do that anymore. The retainer would be tightened every week or two to keep the alignment process on track. This was done with a metal tool that was put into a wheel located in the center of the retainer. My dad had some people over to watch a football game and decided to show everyone how this process worked. He had me lay down on an ottoman in the middle of the room, encircled by onlookers. I had no reason not to trust my dad at this point, so I followed his commands. He told me to open my mouth and proceeded to pour beer into my mouth until I gagged and choked. The room erupted in laughter, and I quickly sat up, dusting myself off and scattering away to hide and cry. Was this why I became an addict? Because I was sensitive to public humiliation?

I never felt comfortable in my own skin. Something was off inside of me. I was unable to be alone with my thoughts for even a second. I needed constant stimulation to distract me from this chaotic internal state. My mom worked a lot, and my dad usually traveled the country recruiting players for his job. I craved the pres-ence of anyone, whether good or bad. As a teenager, I invested time in friendships and valued them over my family. I craved solace in friendships that I wasn't finding at home. One thing I recognized early on was my instinct to avoid danger. Being an observer, I was hyper-aware of my surroundings and would adjust accordingly. I hated confrontation and would steer clear of it at any cost. There was anxiety and fear constantly buzzing in my head. The first time I smoked weed, that steady buzz went away. The quiet I felt in my mind was like driving under an overpass in a heavy rainstorm. For a split second, driving at high speed, there was clarity. Naturally, I fit in with the stoners. I perceived them to be less judgmental and, more importantly, non-confrontational. The more I smoked weed with my friends, the safer I felt away from my dad at home. I was extremely sensitive and emotional, and I had finally found a way to shut all that down. The running started early and became habit-forming. I thought I was the only one who felt the way I did, and I was scared to talk about it with anyone. My perception of what a man is supposed to act like was extremely skewed. I would get so angry at how my dad handled his feelings. He would have short rage fits and then be okay five minutes later. I learned from him that anger should be short-lived. The problem was my anger would last for longer, and I thought something was wrong with me.

I experimented with drugs like a lot of teenagers do, mainly hallucinogens and ecstasy. At the time, I fully believed that these experiences opened my mind to a world unseen to most. I felt more connected and in tune with the world. I was unlocking different levels of understanding and wanted to keep going until everything was revealed. Everything was so new and fresh that it was invigorating at the deepest levels. There was a polar shift in my thinking after the motorcycle accident. I wanted everything to be shut off and halted. I wasn't interested in the world anymore; my emotions were turned up so loud that I couldn't hear anything around me.

It was a blistering summer day, and I was giddy with excitement about acquiring my new street bike. I rode around town, coming up with places to go just so I could ride. My girlfriend had recently broken up with me, and I was doing everything in my power to run away from that feeling. I decided to do my normal rounds of dropping off bags of weed to people around town. I loaded up my airtight jar in a backpack and set off, not expecting that my life would change forever in a few short hours. My last stop was to pick up some cocaine before I headed home for the day. I sat in a motel doing lines with a buddy, trying my best to blot out the reality of my daughter's mom leaving me. I was hopeful as I talked to my friend and even joked about how dangerous street bikes can be to ride. I slid the small baggie into my phone cover to conceal it, just in case I got pulled over. I got on my Yamaha R6 and remember the feeling of the seat burning my skin through my shorts. I wiped my nose clean, put my helmet on, and raced toward the moment that would change my life forever.

I turned on Disc Boulevard heading towards Sparks Boulevard, and everything went black. I don't remember anything from the crash; it was short video clips of consciousness. I woke up staring at a beige metal roof and could hear a steady beep off to the side. I looked around the metal box and noticed a man in a police uniform sitting by my feet. I finally realized I was in an ambulance and felt the steady sway back and forth. I couldn't comprehend how I got there, and my eyes fixated on the officer shaking my airtight jar. He calmly said, "I'm not going to charge you for this because you are really fucked up right now."

"Thank you," I muttered, and the lights went out again.

The next time I opened my eyes, there was a surgeon upside down standing above my head. The room was blindingly bright, and I was straining my eyes to figure out where I was. I combed the inside of my mouth with my tongue and discovered huge gaps in several places.

"Tell me how many teeth I'm missing!" I screamed at the doctor.

"None," he replied. "You're not missing any."

"Bullshit, I can feel the gaps. Just tell me!"

"Look, you're not missing any, your jaw is separated in three places, and I'm going to fix it."

The darkness swallowed me whole. My eyes opened, focusing on a white tile roof, and I knew I was in a hospital bed. As I struggled to put the pieces together, I scanned my surroundings, looking for a familiar face. I went to move my right arm, and nothing happened. This moment was the single most terrifying second of my life. I burst into tears at the thought of being paralyzed from the neck down. My mom comforted me at that moment. While I was in and out of consciousness, I had this hideous dream that I was trapped at the bottom of the ocean. I was held down by something heavy and was struggling to fight my way through a thick patch of seaweed. I could hear my mom calling my name, but I couldn't find her. The more I thrashed, the weaker I got. I finally gave up and stopped the battle. I started to float toward the surface, and everything felt sublime. I woke up as soon as I accepted my fate. I realized later how similar this fight was to my battle with addiction. Everything got easier once I stopped fighting everything and everyone.

I now know the experience left me at a crossroads in my life, and I chose the wrong path. The pain was deeper than physical or emotional, my spirit was ripped in half, and I was willing to do anything to escape it. That accident caused a spiritual death inside of me, and I underestimated how long it would take to heal.

Chapter Three

Shattered: Lisa

"Faith is the strength by which a
shattered world shall emerge into the light."
Helen Keller

There was a time I was oblivious to the ravages of addiction and to the possibility it would weave itself into our family. The tragedies that unfolded on the news or in casual conversations seemed so far away. The formula was always the same, addicts got sober or died of an overdose. I was naïve to the in-between, the parts where the continuous heartaches happen. When it happened to us, I realized there were many things to be afraid of because using drugs was only the beginning. It brings with it a set of problems that are just as unimaginable as the addiction itself.

I thought about a conversation I had with a trauma doctor as I stood in front of my son, his right arm hanging by his side, the hand scabbed and oozing. "An infection in the upper extremity is so dangerous because it has a direct pathway to the heart. I've seen heroin addicts wheeled into the ER dead, killed by an untreated infection that started at the injection site." There were many ways I imagined Gerad could die: overdose, HIV, hypothermia, but an infection had not been one of them. By this time, he had tried to get sober twice and failed. I had asked him to leave after each relapse, so he was moving around a lot. I tracked him down at a local motel. In our last call, he had told me he had found a couple of guys to rent a hotel room with near downtown. He even told me the name, but it didn't ring a bell, and I couldn't place it. There is a cluster of rundown motels along 4th Street in Reno, and I figured that was the most likely place I would find him. I was right.

Drive on the outskirts of any downtown, and you will see the same cluster of motels that have seen better days. Once shining symbols, they opened travel to the middle class who could park their pride-and-joy sedan or station wagon at the front door of their room at the "motor lodge." Airline tickets were out of reach, as were the hotels that stood in the downtowns of most major cities. Clean and simple, with "air conditioning" and "television" advertised on their neon signs, they were safe and affordable. Few remnants of those glory days exist now. They have become housing for families that couldn't manage to scrape together the security and utility deposits needed for an apartment. They were the place of last resort for seniors that had to make a choice between staying in their homes or being able to buy food and medications. And they were home to drifters and addicts, at least for a night or two, since they were the only place you could rent until the money ran out; no lease required. I had driven by these motels every day and couldn't recall a single name. Driving by them now, I paid attention. Sunset Lodge, Wildflower Lodge, El Tavern Motor Inn, trying to remember the name Gerad had given me. It was hard to imagine anyone choosing to pull in, let alone stay in one of these places now. I just had a general impression that they were a place for people that had nowhere else to go, and that fit Gerad's situation perfectly.

When I first found out about Gerad's heroin use, I moved him into the casita on our property. He had become a couch surfer in his own home, a place my mother owned, where he had previously lived with his girlfriend and daughter. After their break-up, his motorcycle accident, and subsequent surgery, things got progressively worse. By the time I understood what was going on, the place had become a crash pad for whoever could supply the drugs. I was furious, kicked everyone out, and began throwing away the junk that had accumulated from all the drifters. I had no idea, even then, how bad things had gotten. Not when people showed up claiming they needed to grab their stuff, or when the couple staying in one of the bedrooms locked themselves in and refused to leave, and not even when, for the next few days, that same couple would break in through the window to have a place to sleep. At first, I believed him when Gerad claimed that he knew they were using heroin and that the drug paraphernalia wasn't his. He played the victim very well. When I came across cabinets full of aluminum foil, I even commented on how "pissed off " all the freeloaders would be that their stash was gone. I didn't ask him if he wanted to leave; I just packed his stuff, loaded what we could carry in the car, and drove him to my house. I honestly thought I was rescuing him from what his life had become and the people that were taking advantage of him. He finally admitted he was using too.

Of course, moving him out of there didn't stop his drug use, so we began a cycle of taking him in, multiple attempts to get clean, and then kicking him out when we caught him using. So began the succession of weekly motels when he could scrape up the money, or mom guilt took over, and I ended up paying for a couple of nights. I received an eye-opening tour of places I had never even noticed, let alone been to, yet they served as an important fail-safe for the indigent, the minimum wage worker, and addicts. And now they were the sometimes home for my son.

There are moments of great despair and the feeling of being completely overwhelmed when addiction creeps into your life. I tried to place it all away in a box in my head, but the visits to dark places and the things that lurked there took a toll. I tried to keep the everyday world of work, friends, and family at the forefront so I wouldn't be consumed with worry and guilt, but it always showed up in the droop of my shoulders, the slump of my back, and the circles under my eyes. I didn't recognize my own son and still couldn't understand how we had gotten to this point. The thoughts crept in a hundred times a day, and I worked hard to push them away, but I couldn't control the nights. The nights were the worst, and it was during those sleepless nights that I would decide to go drive around and find him.

Although I had driven around looking for Gerad in the evenings and weekends, searching for him on my way to work wasn't a usual thing. As I drove toward work that Tuesday and passed those motels, I told myself that I would just take a quick detour through the parking lots, but I wouldn't stop unless, of course, I saw his car. I had driven through three lots before I reached the Desert Rose Inn. The name did not suit the place. The only thing "rosy" about the place was its pink paint and even darker pink trim. It was two stories with an office at the front of the property as you entered the parking lot. At first glance, and compared to the other motels I had driven by, it didn't look that bad. If you looked closely, however, you could see that the paint was fading, the sign no longer functioned, and every single room had the curtains drawn. It was eerily quiet, a place people went to disappear for a while. There was a pool no one had bothered to fill, it appeared, in years. The parking lot was surprisingly full. Either I had been way off base on who stayed here, or there were more desperate people in Reno than I had imagined. I felt embarrassed by my lack of awareness. I spotted Gerad's car and pulled in close by. I decided to knock on a few doors closest to where his car was parked.

The easiest way to describe what I looked like that morning was out of place. I would by no means stick out in most places dressed for work in a suit and heels, but I was out of place now as I pulled up in my late-model SUV. I'm sure it would raise red flags for the motel occupants, but I was on a mission. As I shut off my car, a few curtains parted, a single eye staring out. Without considering how absurd I looked or the possibility this was dangerous, I knocked on the door closest to Gerad's car. From the outside, all the rooms looked alike, with a nondescript door and a double sliding window to the left. Cigarette butts were strewn on the concrete in front of the rooms, and the concrete was cracked with small weeds protruding out of the openings. Other than the ants that had taken up residence in the sidewalk cracks, nothing else was moving aside from the occasional curtain. I'm pretty sure I wasn't who the occupants were expecting, so those curtains closed as quickly as they opened. No one answered, so I knocked again. I could see a slight rustling of the curtains as if someone had gotten up from the bed and headed to the door. After one more knock, I gave up and moved on to the next room. This time the door was opened by a stocky guy in his 20s with dark hair and holding the leash of a Mastiff. The light from the room behind him was a yellowish glow, and I could see the outline of several other people lying on the bed, one slumped against the wall and someone standing behind him. I counted in my head that there were five people and a dog in one small room. That was a punch to the gut. Not what I envisioned when Gerad said he was sharing a room with a couple of guys. He had only cracked the door partway, so I brought my face closer and told him I was looking for Gerad. He eyed me suspiciously, so I said, "I'm his mom. I just need to talk to him." The door closed without him saying a word. I stood there for a minute, not sure what to do. As I began to head to the next room, the door opened again, and Gerad walked out.

I never got used to how Gerad looked when he was using. It was always a shock but one I never let show. I always felt he was like a scared bird that would take flight if I showed any emotion, shock, elation, or anything. He deliberately walked me away from the room and into the parking lot. As I walked behind him, I took a quick inventory. His clothes were wrinkled and looked as if they hadn't been washed in a while. Apparently, laundry service wasn't part of this motel's amenities. Humor finds its way into the darkest moments, a survival mechanism. You either laugh or cry. His hair was greasy, and he walked slowly, slightly tilting to the right. I couldn't remember noticing that before and realized it was his right shoulder that sloped, a result of his motorcycle accident. Although surgery had restored movement to his right arm, it had not worked to restore movement in his shoulder, and the muscles had atrophied, giving the appearance of his right arm hanging down lower than his left. Although he had made it to a few visits, he had long abandoned physical therapy to strengthen the muscles. He had lost weight, and his jeans were baggy. He had shoes on but no socks. The shoes were past the point anyone else would have kept them, but I guess they served their purpose for Gerad.

He slowed and then stopped in the parking lot. I asked how he was doing, and he rambled for a few minutes about looking for work and being happy he found a room to share. He was squinting into the sun, and I realized he hadn't been out in the daylight in a while. He was greyer than pale, with dark circles under his eyes. The idea that he was looking for work in this condition was laughable. Gerad wanted me to believe his situation hadn't affected his ability to get a job or find a place to stay; you know, everything was normal. I rarely challenged him. It was part of the game. I was trying not to scare him off, and he was trying not to scare me. I looked down at his right hand. He had been fighting an infection in it for a year. When it first formed an abscess, he had gone to HOPES, a community health clinic, and they had lanced it and put him on antibiotics. He had called and told me he went for help because he had a fever and swelling in his arm. He had been proud of the fact he had taken care of it. The clinic was a safe place for addicts to go with no judgment, and with the only needle exchange program in Reno, it was a lifesaver for Gerad and many others.

I have many friends who believe a needle exchange program promotes drug use or coddles addicts. It is a narrow view and misses the bigger issue. Addiction is a game of Russian roulette; the barrel keeps spinning, and you never know when the bullet is coming that will take your child away. You do everything you can to keep them alive long enough to get sober, and if a clean needle prevents an infection like HIV or hepatitis that can kill them, it should be available everywhere. Everything you thought to be true before dealing with this insidious disease gets flipped on its head when it's your child. I found myself no longer discussing Gerad with those who couldn't understand, but it is exactly what needs to happen. If we could talk about it openly without shame, judgment, and especially without people's political platitudes, we may be able to save lives.

He was supposed to go back to the clinic for follow-ups which, judging by the look of his hand now, he had never done, coupled with the fact he just kept injecting into the site. I doubted he had ever taken the antibiotics they gave him. When Gerad was young, he had a very low pain tolerance. He would run to show me every scrape and bruise, insisting on a Band-Aid. I could usually sympathize and kiss the boo-boo and make it better. He was sensitive in so many ways, and pain was no exception. We were way beyond a Band-Aid now, and no kiss would make it better. I wanted to take him in my arms and hug him. I wanted to take his pain away. Instead, I stood completely still, keeping the distance between us, barely breathing. Having Gerad in front of me was becoming fewer and farther between, and I was paralyzed. He was an adult. I couldn't raise my voice, and I couldn't threaten to ground him. All his choices were his.

I glanced down at his hand again and the gaping wounds. It was hard not to stare. This was the same hand that had produced such imaginative art, the same hand that had cradled his daughter's head the day she was born, and the same hand that held mine so often as a young boy. It looked so painful. I assumed he would choose another place to shoot up; then I realized he couldn't feel it. Although the use of his motor nerves had been restored to his hand, he had never regained his sensory nerves, making it the perfect place to inject. The downside was he couldn't feel the pain caused by the infection until it was moving up his arm. I couldn't help but think of all he had gone through with his accident, the surgery to restore movement, the physical therapy, and trips to Rochester just to have his arm and hand end up like this. I can't imagine a greater waste of a miracle. I decided I had to give it my best shot, "Gerad, you're going to lose that hand, best case scenario or the infection is going to move to your heart and kill you." It was the most direct conversation I had ever had with him surrounding his addiction. He unconsciously grabbed the arm and rubbed it, looking at the ground. I asked if I could take a picture of it and show it to one of the doctors. He slowly held it out, and I snapped a photo with my cell phone. I still have it.

He looked back toward the room, and I could tell he felt uncomfortable. He wanted me to leave in a protective way. He didn't want me to see the reality of his living conditions or his physical condition. It was the unspoken lie between us. "I'll be fine." This was still early on in our journey, but it was a turning point. There was still a sad innocence about how far he was into this downward spiral and how long this journey would be for us all. I wanted to throw up or scream and take him back home and take care of him. I was losing him. There was no reasoning that could get through to him. I told him I would show the picture to a doctor and that he needed to take care of it. He was getting fidgety and anxious with the conversation. He kept unconsciously grabbing and rubbing the hand. He was relieved when I told him I had to go. I wanted him to say, "Don't leave," or "Take me with you." Instead, he turned and walked back toward the room. I called out one last time, "The offer still stands. If you want to get clean, I'll take you anytime, anywhere." He smiled sadly and said, "I love you, Mom." I wanted to shatter into a million pieces.

A few days later, he would take me up on the offer. It would be his third attempt. I had tried to call him to let him know the doctor felt it was urgent he get treatment for his infection. The call went straight to voicemail; his voicemail was full. He called me later from a number I didn't recognize. He told tell me he had lost his phone or it had been stolen. It was always the same story, and I lost track of which one it was this time. I knew he had traded it for drugs. A cell phone is your only lifeline to an addict, so without one, you never know if they are alive or dead. I think of all those cell phones sold and traded, strewn in a big pile at the dump; one last thing they gave up for heroin and their last connection to the life they knew before it. I saw a saying once, "Addiction is giving up everything for one thing." Several times I got him a new phone in hopes he would stay in contact, but it never lasted long. I always answered numbers I didn't recognize, which I had never done before, just in case it was Gerad. I asked how he was and how his hand felt. He never called just to check in anymore. He usually reached out when things got bad: cold weather, hunger, sickness, or jail. I guessed this time he called because he no longer had money to pay his part of the room or buy heroin and hoped going to detox was better than getting dope sick on the street. He didn't ask for help, so I focused on the hand rather than the addiction. I told him I would pick him up in the morning at 6:00 am in the Desert Rose parking lot. If he was outside, I'd take him for help, and if he wasn't, I'd keep driving. He was quiet for a bit, then said, "I'll be outside."

I never gave up hope that Gerad would get help, so I went to pick him up, praying he would be there but prepared if he didn't show. It wouldn't be the first time. There are so many disappointments and so many rock bottoms. You drop the bar lower and lower, holding at just keeping them alive. You no longer flinch at things that would have once seemed unfathomable before your world changed, and acceptance and prayer were all you had left.

As I pulled into the parking lot, it was still dark out, and I didn't see him. My heart sank for the millionth time. I drove past the office and turned left, moving further into the parking lot. Nothing. I glanced in my rearview mirror and saw movement. I hit the brakes. Gerad walked out from between two cars. My heart skipped a beat, and I held my breath until he was settled in the passenger seat and I put the car in drive. The hopefulness I felt at that moment would be dashed in the weeks to come, but for now, it was enough.

Chapter Three

Shattered: Gerad

"He who lives by the crystal ball
shall eat shattered glass."
Ray Dalio

There was a time when I was terrified of needles, and I whole-heartedly believed that I would never use one. When I started using heroin, I smoked it off foil. I had many conversations with addicts, and they always told me, "It's not a matter of if but when." I would emphatically argue that I would never be that guy, but something drastically changed in my mind after the surgery when I realized that there wasn't much improvement. All bets were off. In my mind's eye was an image of myself trapped in a shattered mirror, and there was no way back to my previous self, my whole self.

I remember the first time that I used a needle. I filled the syringe with cooked-down heroin and held it in my hand, staring at it for at least 10 minutes. The sun was setting and pierced through the vertical blinds, focusing light on the choice I was about to make. Somehow, I knew this wouldn't be just one time. How did my life get to this point? I knew deep down that once this bridge was crossed, there was no turning back. I poked and prodded myself for an hour trying to figure out how this process even worked. Ironically my numb arm made this a painless learning experience. I wonder now if I would have kept trying if I could feel what I was doing to myself. If only I had directed that determination to mending myself and finding a way forward, I could have had a chance, but my only goal at this point was to get as high as possible with whatever I could get my hands on and escape. When I pulled the trigger, I had no idea my life would be put on hold for a decade.

When that threshold was crossed, things deteriorated quickly. At the time, I was still staying in the house my grandmother had bought to give me a safe space for what had been my family: my girlfriend, my daughter, and me. After the accident, I stopped paying rent. I didn't have much else to offer. She must have felt bad for me as so many others did during this time. I always used that to my advantage.

Before the accident, I had spent quite a few years selling weed, working at a golf resort, and going to school. I thought I had a lot of friends, but after my motorcycle accident, things were much different. I had burned all the bridges I had in the weed game after someone stole a large amount from my house. My buddy offered me a front to get back on my feet, and I decided it would be a better idea to buy opiates with the money instead of paying him back. My selfishness was endless. My house quickly became a revolving door of addicts and dealers that were looking for a place to crash for a couple of nights. I used the room and board to my advantage and was able to keep my high going consistently. I learned better ways to get high from people that were in the same boat as me—a boat that drifted out to sea with no paddles or fresh water. I felt close to these people at the time, mainly because we spent a lot of time together, but I learned how fickle "friendships" were in this world. People were only around for as long as the drugs were. I carried the same point of view. If you had nothing to offer, then you'd better leech somewhere else. The world became cold, dark, and ever shifting.

My mom was suspicious of my behavior for a while and would call periodically to see how I was doing. I told her what she wanted to hear to keep her as far away as possible. I couldn't hide from her forever. She eventually came over and saw the situation I was in. I will never forget the look on her face when I told her I was doing heroin for the first time. When I was three years old, I was out helping my dad spray the vehicles off in the driveway. Our dog was out front with us on a chain, and I was standing on it, oblivious, as I sprayed the hose. When my dog spotted another dog, she took off running and ripped my feet out from under me. I smacked my head on the concrete extremely hard. The only thing I remember from this incident is my mother holding me in the car on the way to the hospital. The look on her face was the exact same as when I told her I was shooting heroin. Completely helpless. There was so much pain behind her eyes. These were the only times I saw my mom utterly terrified. My world was shattering like a windshield hit by a rock; the cracks were everywhere. I never wanted to break my mom's heart or disappoint my family. I would have stopped right there if this wasn't such an insidious disease.

When I first attempted to get clean, I believed that I could do it. I would have passed a lie detector test with flying colors. The problem was that I wasn't doing it for myself. It was merely a response to my mom's reaction. I wanted to get clean for my daughter, my mom, and my brothers, and that was insane. I convinced myself that I would be happy if I could make them all proud of me. So, I gave it a shot. I detoxed for the first time at my mom's house, and it was miserable. The runny nose, vomiting, shitting my guts out, restless legs, uncontrollable yawns, and watery eyes. I finally got some relief when my mom took me to see a psychiatrist who prescribed me Suboxone. I jumped through the hoops and took them as prescribed for a couple of weeks. My mom monitored me to the best of her ability while working a full-time job. I felt like an empty shell drifting like a tumbleweed with no destination. I had no spiritual guidance and could feel myself being driven toward heroin's relief. I soon started selling the Suboxone. Heroin was the security blanket that took it all away, especially the guilt and shame of being a bad son/father. I hid it for maybe a couple of days before my mom called me out on it, and just like that, I had my excuse to disappear again. This delusion that I was smarter than everyone around me became a constant problem. I acted like they were crazy when I got caught, and I would make a huge scene and storm out. The emotional terrorism was my trump card to justify everything. That image of my mom's terrified face was gone; it was like it had never happened.

The only thing I had of value at this time was my vehicle. As you can imagine, not many addicts can afford a car. I stayed on different couches and helped dealers deliver their drugs in hopes of some scraps falling on the floor. The power that heroin dealers had made me nauseous. The world moved at their pace, and you were at the mercy of their schedule. It was hard enough to scrounge together enough money to get me through the day and a whole different level of stress begging these people to meet you in a timely fashion. This cat-and-mouse game took up most of my day. They would tell me to meet in a parking lot at a certain time and never show up. I would call, desperate for them to give me what I needed, but they would string me along for hours on end. It was like having the flu 24 hours a day and trying to track the medication down throughout the city. My life became a constant struggle, and nothing was ever guaranteed. I got to know the motels of Reno very well. I knew what to find, where, and who had it. If my fellow degenerates and I had the money, we would get a room for a couple of nights. This was luxury living at its finest. Motels were easy because they never asked questions. They weren't exactly doing background checks to fill up their rooms. If you paid, they left you alone. The Desert Rose was a staple for my housing. It was mainly for the location more than the aesthetics. This was a one-stop shop for everything you could need. I got a room with a guy around my age and stayed there for several weeks. The living conditions were dismal, to say the least. No one showered, and the guy had a dog staying with us. I'm sure the smell was as putrid as a locker room on a summer's day. I got several abscesses on my hand and arm while staying there due to the poor conditions. I wasn't exactly sterilizing my equipment on a regular basis. If we had only one needle, we would each take turns bleaching out the inside and hoping for the best. Thank God for the needle exchange in Reno. That place made me feel like I was human, and they looked me in the eye when they were talking to me. They gently walked me through the process of treating an abscess and educated me on how dangerous they can be. They provided clean needles, sterile water, and other necessitates for keeping people somewhat on track. The most important function of this place was the testing and treatment of diseases and how to care for abscesses. The Northern Nevada HOPES clinic saves thousands of lives. There should be one of these in every city across the country.

My mom always had great timing. She showed up, unannounced, at the room I was staying in at the Desert Rose. My right arm was swollen and oozing from so many holes; a dart board in a dive bar had fewer holes in it. My eyes were yellow, and I was peeing a dark brown color. These are the telltale signs of hepatitis. Mom came knocking on the door, and I was so relieved and scared at the same time. I gave her the usual song and dance about how I was going to figure my way out of this phase. I was terrified to tell her the truth, and I wish I had been honest from the beginning. I wanted her to be proud of me, and I could see the pain in her eyes every time she saw me. I lied because I didn't want to hurt her anymore. She pointed out the condition of my arm, and I told her about the other symptoms I was having. Reality set in for a quick moment; I feared death for the first time since my accident. I decided to go with her the next morning to detox. Maybe the fear of death will work this time.

Chapter Four

Fourteen Days: Lisa

"There are no problems,
only solutions"
John Lennon

Heroin was holding us all hostage. Our lives and our time were no longer our own. We were stuck in an endless cycle of disappointments. I had become a slave to the fear of losing Gerad, and I couldn't see a way out of doing anything and everything to keep him alive.

The hoops you must jump through to end up nowhere are maddening, and the system is full of ironies. To be accepted into a treatment program in Nevada, you need two things: an assessment to prove you are truly in need of help and to be clean at the time of admission. That means finding a place to detox. So here we were, filling out the paperwork for another $100 assessment which basically consists of a series of questions to verify you're an addict and you are open to recovery. This was our third time. The questions struck me as almost polite and not meant in any way to determine who was in imminent danger. More for the businessman who had two too many martinis at business lunches, not my homeless heroin addict that gambled with his life every day.

Question one: "Has your performance at school, work, or home been affected by your drug or alcohol use?"

"Are you kidding me," I wanted to scream. "He doesn't have a home, go to school, or work. Look at him! I'm trying to save his life, not his job!" Yet here we were once again playing the game. I sat in the small waiting room, wondering why these assessments were necessary. Why would someone choose to go to a recovery program if they were not an addict? Turns out the DSM or, *Diagnostic and Statistical Manual of Mental Disorders* specifies to make a diagnosis of addiction requires a person to have seven to eleven specific symptoms. No official diagnosis and no rehab bed. I would like to believe that with limited beds, those in the greatest need would be chosen, yet an alcoholic with a job, insurance, and family support is the most likely to get in. Unfortunately, hardcore addicts are rarely that lucky. By the time the family has convinced them to go to rehab, they have no bank account and nothing of value, let alone insurance coverage for a program. Rehab is rarely their idea. Logically, since there are so few beds available, I'd believed they used these assessments to pick those in the worst shape until I heard the questions. It's like playing God. How can you possibly know who is one hit away from an overdose?

What they don't tell you is the assessment is only good for 30 days. So, if you can find your couch surfing—or worse, homeless— child on the streets and convince them to consider a program, you spend the first ten days trying to get an appointment at a place that does the assessments and hoping you can locate your kid once you do. Reliability is not an addict's strong suit. Assuming you successfully complete the assessment, you spend the next two weeks calling the detox centers daily, begging for an intake interview, which can't be scheduled unless there is an available bed. Slowly you learn the right things to say to get in the door. If that's successful and they decide your child is in enough danger to be accepted, the addict spends two weeks in detox. All the while, you are calling programs to see if you can get them in one before their discharge date. Once out of detox, you let the programs know he is ready, and they tell you he must have another assessment before he can be accepted.

On a positive note, a few programs will schedule over-the-phone assessments. I had one program bill me for two phone assessments even though they never accepted him into their program within their own 30-day rule. If you can get an assessment that hasn't expired and find a bed for detox, there is no program to take him anyway, so the merry-go-round keeps spinning. Pretty quickly, you give up on programs and assessments and just try to convince them to detox, and you'll figure out the rest later—it's 14 days you know they'll remain alive.

The first time I got Gerad into a detox facility was in 2014, three years after his accident and one year after finding out about his addiction. It was his third attempt to get clean but his first in a medically assisted detox facility. Two prior attempts without medically supervised detox had failed. He had called me from a pay phone late at night and asked if I would pick him up. He said he was tired of being tired and wanted to go into detox. I never gave up hope that he meant it no matter how many times I had heard those words, so I told him to stay put and I would get him. As I got in my car, I prayed he would still be there. I pulled into the convenience store/gas station and could see him sitting on the curb. He looked exhausted. He got in and told me he was going to try to walk to my house but couldn't go any further. He had found some change on the ground and called me. I took him home, and he showered and lay down in bed. I hoped he would be there in the morning, which was only a few hours away.

I started calling places at 8 am in between going in and out to check on Gerad. I could tell he was wavering on going. I felt desperate. By noon I had gotten nowhere and had to show up to work at some point. This would be the second time he agreed to try and get clean, but the first time using a medical facility. Detoxing at home without medical assistance had been excruciating, and neither he nor I was willing to go through that again. I enlisted my mother. She had been in sales and seemed to be able to convince anyone of anything. While I went to work, she put her sales skills to work.

From each call I had made that morning, I figured out the right answers to their questions, so I gave her instructions on how to play the game: "Yes, he was homeless because of his drug use. Yes, he was in full withdrawals. Symptoms: pain all over his body, stomach pain, vomiting, and diarrhea. Drug of choice: heroin and whatever else he could get his hands on, Xanax, meth, and Valium. Willingness to detox? Very high. Understood that he would be kept here for up to three weeks? Of course, he is ready." In reality, I wasn't sure I would even get him in the car and to the door of the facility without him bolting, but I'd figure it out. There's a lot of figuring it out on the fly to get them in the door of a place that may just give you a few days to catch your breath before you start the process all over again.

My mom called me at 3:45 pm and said that if I could get him to the detox facility by 4:30 pm, they had agreed to interview him. An interview didn't guarantee admission but based on the condition he was in, I figured they would take him. I just hoped he was still where I had left him. At that time, in our community, most detox facilities were behavioral hospitals dealing with mental health issues. There were no facilities specific to addiction. These facilities were created to prevent those with mental health emergencies from harming themselves. The beds were divided for either mental health or detox. Due to staffing, mission, and expertise, there were always more of the former than the latter. The ratio hadn't changed to keep up with the growing demand for detox, so the chances of getting admitted were slim. Gerad was still in bed when I told him he had an interview. I could tell by the way he looked at me he had second thoughts. I found my husband and told him I wasn't sure I could get him there. He walked into the room and told him to "get his ass up," and a few seconds later, Gerad walked out and got into my car. Apparently, getting right to the point worked.

We pulled up in front of a nondescript building built for function, not beauty. I'm sure whoever designed it figured a person in the middle of a mental health crisis wouldn't pay much attention to aesthetics. Flat roofline, brown brick with beige trim, fencing around the entire circumference, and two wings that jutted out from the middle reception area. It didn't inspire confidence. I had never noticed this place even though I had lived here for 17 years. The reception area was small, with industrial tile on the floors, fluorescent lighting, and armless plastic chairs. I expected an odor, but it was strangely odorless, with stale air that made the room stuffy. A television was mounted in the corner tuned to the Food Network. The receptionist was behind bulletproof glass, and there was a tray at the bottom of the window that popped out like a bank teller. I gave them his name, but she couldn't find an appointment.

"Don told us to be here by 4:30, and he would interview him," I told her.

She hustled through the locked door in the back of her space and disappeared. I glanced at Gerad and couldn't tell if he looked relieved, hoping we could leave, or annoyed. To even be considered for an interview, you must be in full withdrawal and "sick enough" for admission. Gerad's complexion was blueish grey, with blackened circles for eye sockets. His lips were dry, and he kept licking them, but his mouth was also dry, so his tongue kept sticking to the roof of his mouth and making a sucking sound as it released. He was getting fidgety. We were still standing next to the entrance door, and I watched him glance outside. I asked him to go ahead and sit down. I realized he didn't want to be here and was doing this for me. Despite my heart feeling like it was beating out of my chest, I tried to remain calm. Even though you get used to constant disappointment, when you've gotten this far, it would be hard to swallow to be told to leave. The minutes ticked by. You get used to failure as the mother of an addict. You hear "no" so many times you begin to wonder what you are doing wrong. Turns out you're fighting an ill-equipped system that doesn't know how to support you. I was expecting her to come back and tell me there'd been a mistake, but as she opened the door, she made eye contact which I took as a good sign. "You can have a seat."

We sat down against the back wall under a high narrow window. The entire building had high narrow windows; I assumed to prevent people from escaping. It struck me as ironic that I was begging them to allow him in, and yet there were enough people trying to escape that the only windows were too high to reach. In the waiting area, there was a middle-aged man with a girl that looked to be 20 or so. A red-haired woman sat alone on the other side of the room. There is a veneer the mothers of addicts' wear. You recognize it in those that sit in the many reception areas you end up in looking for help. The longer they have been in this battle, the thicker the veneer. You hope for the best but expect the worst.

The only door in the room opened, and the man and girl were called back. I had no idea how this would work. I hadn't thought about whether I would be part of the interview. I hadn't thought about anything but getting him here. That's how it works; you try so hard to get them to a safe place, but you don't think about what happens next. One night off the streets, one day out of jail, one day still alive. I glanced over at Gerad, who had his head tilted back, eyes closed, and his hands folded on his lap. He had shrunk, his clothes were baggy, and his skin slack. I glanced over at the television, closed my eyes, and prayed this worked.

The door opened. A balding man with kind eyes said, "Gerrard," the common mispronunciation of Gerad's name. I asked if I could come, and he turned to Gerad and asked if he was OK with it. Gerad nodded without glancing back. He escorted us into a common area with what I assumed were four interview rooms around it. The room straight ahead was empty, and he directed us to sit in the same orange plastic chairs that adorned the waiting room, but this time they surrounded a small table. He didn't close the door, and I could see directly across into another interview room. The young girl I had seen in the waiting room was slumped in her chair, crying as the interviewer seemed to be trying to convince her to stay. Honestly, I had no idea what they were saying, but I welcomed the distraction, wondering if that family was going through something worse than ours. Our interviewer was Don. He was soft-spoken and asked each question with deep concern. I had expected judgment and disinterest, but Don was respectful and asked the questions in language that was familiar to Gerad. Gerad answered the questions mechanically, but he at least answered the questions. There was a window, lower than the others in the building, that I could look out of. It had bars across it, and I hoped Gerad didn't notice. I stared out of it as Gerad went through the last time he used, what he used, how much he was using a day, how many sexual partners he had, what his withdrawal symptoms were, where he was staying, and his medical history. It was heart-wrenching to hear. I felt as sick as Gerad looked. You learn early on to stay still and quiet even as you deal with the most surreal experiences of your life. I was holding my breath, hoping he was answering the questions in a way that would result in his admission. THEY HAD TO KEEP HIM. I was silently screaming. Don had obviously done these many times before Gerad. He carefully prodded, lowering Gerad's anxiety and letting him know that there was no judgment. Truthful answers would help them help him. "How old are you, Gerad? How old were you when you started using?"

My mind wandered back to a day in a park when Gerad had just turned four. He was running from the swings to the slide and asked his brother how old he was.

"Four!" Ryan answered.

"No, I not, I free," Gerad said.

They yelled back and forth, "Yes you are," "No I not," and then Gerad yelled from across the park, "Mommy, how old am I?"

"Gerad, you're four," I said.

"NO, I NOT I FREEEEE!"

I wish he was three again or free. I wish we were both free of this disease.

As the interview concluded, Don asked if Gerad had any questions for him. He shook his head. Don said he would talk to his supervisor and see if he would approve his admission. He explained that they only had so many beds for detox, and they were currently full. He said he'd see what he could do. Addicts are put into tiers both for detox and program admission. Pregnant women come first; they're admitted automatically and always seem to find a bed in a program. Intravenous heroin users come next, check. For detox, you must be in full-blown withdrawals. If your symptoms aren't serious enough, no admission. I had told him on the way over to be honest about all his withdrawal symptoms. Looking at him now, I don't think he had to play up anything. He was sick. Really, really sick.

I watched Don disappear into a side door that appeared to have offices behind it. I could see him through a window standing next to a desk, talking to someone I couldn't see. He walked back through the common area without glancing our way. I took that as a bad sign. The young girl across the way was standing up now. I heard her say she wasn't suicidal. The man had his arm around her. I don't know if that meant they had convinced her to stay or if she was leaving. At least she had a choice. I just wanted a chance.

We had been here for two hours, and still no word. I was hoping Don was working some magic behind the scenes and not that we had been forgotten. He popped his head in and asked if Gerad had any insurance. I had signed him up on Medicaid a few months before. I said it hesitantly since I wasn't sure if they took Medicaid. Gerad was too old to be on our health insurance, and it didn't cover detox or treatment programs anyway. He said he was working on converting a mental health bed into a detox bed and to give him some more time. Someone higher up had to approve the move. I found myself holding my breath again. It was silent in the room. Gerad's eyes were closed, and he was doing his best to gut out his withdrawal. Don came back with papers in hand. Admission had been approved. Gerad opened his eyes. As Don began asking more questions, Gerad became agitated. I don't think he thought this would end in admission. He would go through the motions to make me happy and then leave when there were no beds. Don brought in reinforcements, a lady whose name I didn't catch, that talked Gerad through what would happen next. I also did my best to reassure him, but he looked like he felt trapped. I hadn't come this far to fail now. After what seemed like an eternity of persuasion, he accepted the terms of the admission, and I hugged him goodbye, promising I would be here during every visitation. I turned to leave, trying not to run to the door in case they changed their minds. Fourteen days, I had just bought him fourteen days.

Chapter Four

Fourteen Days: Gerad

"The only difference between a problem
and a solution is that people understand the solution."
Charles Kettering

I had become a slave to this lifestyle. As a kid, I couldn't imagine I'd grow up spending my days walking the streets with no destination. When you're living it, you tell yourself you're just walking to the beat of your own drum, but in reality, it's more like the blip of a flatlined heart monitor. Time doesn't matter; days don't matter, and hygiene doesn't matter. The only important thing is not to get sick. That is the top priority. It's hard to explain what it feels like to walk around aimlessly in the middle of the night with no place to rest. I had no phone to call anyone and no one that would answer if I did. I had no plan to stop using. I had accepted this life and was resigned to the fact that I was going to die like this. Only when I was running out of options would I think about detox, so I was always desperate when I tried.

The first time I considered going to detox was not because I wanted to get sober but because I had nowhere to go and no money to spend. I would say and do anything to manipulate my way into getting what I wanted, so I would go to different motels and knock on doors to see if I could find a place to rest for the night. Reno has a steady buzz at all times of the day and night, so days blend into the evenings with no sense of time. I knocked desperately on a room I was shooting up in earlier that day, but no one answered, even though I could see and hear people in the room. I didn't have anything to offer, I had no money or drugs, and this isn't the life where people offer a helping hand out of the kindness of their hearts. Invisibility is acquired when you become a homeless heroin addict. People stop acknowledging you and avoid eye contact. The shadows were my existence. Before I was an addict, I remember seeing homeless people just walk out into traffic. It's not because they were stupid or incompetent. I believe they were desperate for a glimpse of connection. I believe that because I lived it first-hand.

The night I called my mom to go to detox happened by chance. When I walked, I always kept my eyes glued to the ground. I found things constantly around the city, so that became routine behavior. That night I spotted a quarter and picked it up. A few blocks later, I found two dimes and a nickel. I thought, "50 cents can only buy me one phone call, but who could I call?" My feet were aching and blistered from walking around with no socks on. I found a pay phone, which was no small feat, and started racking my brain to figure out where to get my next fix.

Memory tends to be nonexistent in this state of mind, but I could remember one number, the only number I ever memorized, my mom's. I knew deep down that I couldn't keep walking, and I was so tired of being tired. My gut told me to make the call. I thought, "What if she doesn't answer? When will she draw the line and completely stop talking to me?" I had to try. My mom answered on the second ring. "Mom, can you come pick me up? I'm so tired of walking. I need help." She was always there to rescue me, and I wondered when my chances would run out. She told me she would be there and not to move. I couldn't move if I wanted to. When she picked me up, instantly, I shrank. The ambient green dashboard lit up her look of worry; it was a constant every time I saw her. She looked like a tiny dam trying to hold back the entire ocean. She spoke to me in a very low and soothing tone. I had a history of reacting poorly and making a scene to get my way, so I didn't blame her. I was starting to get sick, and exhaustion overtook me. She took me back to the house to shower, and I was able to actually lay down in a bed for the first time in months and sleep for six hours. It was enough for now.

The mental battle began. I was grateful to be off the street but suspicious of what I would have to do. The truth was, I didn't want to be sober. I couldn't stand the way I felt. I couldn't stand the way I looked. I couldn't stand myself. There I was in this king-sized bed at my mom's house feeling immediately ungrateful. Why did I spend those 50 cents on calling my mom? Why didn't I hold out and find another way? I had lied about wanting to go to detox and knew that I would have to face that reality quickly. In my addicted brain, there were only short windows of willingness where I craved a different life. The idea dissipated like sand through my fingers if I waited too long. My mom and grandma were in and out of the room like a revolving door. They both spoke softly and quickly as if to not scare me away. The only thing I could focus on was the sickness. If I got up, I knew I would hurl, but at the same time, I couldn't sit still.

All I wanted was to get well, but my options were running out. When the negotiations started, I was combative at every turn. I knew going to detox would only extend the excruciating pain I was in. I needed tough love at that moment, and it burst through the door in the form of my stepdad. "GET YOUR ASS UP! YOU'RE GOING TO DETOX!" He accomplished in 10 seconds what my mom and grandma had been trying to do for hours. I quickly jumped up and hurried to my mom's car. My legs were weak and shaky, and I was sweating bullets but cold at the same time. I didn't know what to expect.

I had never been to detox and had no idea what to expect. I remember the sounds and smells more than anything. I kept my eyes closed as much as possible to maintain some sort of balance in my stomach. It was like a hospital because it had very bright lights and smelled like the cleaning aisle of your local grocery store. The creaking of the bathroom door in the waiting room sounded like a rusty wooden barn door. I could hear distant screams and sobbing; it was also a mental health facility. All my senses were heightened tenfold. What stuck out to me was the locked door between the waiting room and the main hall. I knew there was no return once I went past that. Do I really want to trap myself here for weeks? That's what life felt like to me, constantly trying to avoid traps. I always kept my eye out for the nearest exit. You need a contingency plan when living in constant survival mode.

The door opened, and they called us back. It hurt to lift my head, let alone open my eyes. I struggled to stand and enter the hallway. I answered their questions robotically with one mission in mind, not to feel this way. They constantly reassured me that they would give me something if I were sick enough. Don't you see the state I'm in? Why do I have to answer your stupid fucking questions? Hurry up and give me my damn relief. My mom must have been shocked at the information she was learning. "Yes, I am an IV user. Yes, I share needles. Yes, I have done every drug that was in front of me." There is a name for an addict like me: a trash can. I'll dump whatever into my body to change the way I feel.

The whole process was taking longer than I could stomach. My insides were turning outwards. My entire body was shaky. I wanted to get up and run out of the room but remembered the locked doors. The fight or flight response is constantly in play, and impulsive decisions are a must. The interview was finally over, and relief overcame my body. One step closer to getting this damn gorilla off my back.

After saying goodbye to my mom, I am escorted down a few long, white hallways to a small examination room. "Jesus, more hoops to jump through," I thought begrudgingly. They want to help, sure, but this feels like torture. The doctor examined my whole body, looking for abscesses and sores. I am reminded of the carnage IV use has on the body: dehydrated black veins, bruises touching every color of the rainbow, burns and cuts, and swollen organs, things that go unnoticed when getting high in dark alleys. It's hard to deny my unhealthy state under these bright bulbs. There are more tests, more questions, and more signatures. I look at the doctor's prescription pad and wonder if I could get away with writing my own scripts. The doctors approved my physical and the next stop—salvation. I am given a dose of Ativan and sent to a dark room with white bed sheets and a gray wool blanket. "Try to get some rest," the nurse says.

Time slows down when you're dope sick, minutes feel like hours, and it is impossible to find a comfortable position. I am doing the world's slowest acrobatics in bed, tossing and turning, moving at a steady pace. A puddle of sweat is forming beneath me in the bed. I want to run and sleep at the same time. A nurse with short gray hair and thick glasses comes in and explains that I can finally have my first dose of suboxone. Please make this misery stop. I treat it like a glass of water to a dehydrated man, gulping it down before he can finish telling me what to expect. I don't remember anything he said except for telling me that his son was a heroin addict and that he had a strong empathy for me. His words were like a warm blanket smothering the active circus in my head. I realized that he was the first person in a long time who had actually looked me in the eye and treated me like a human being. I missed that feeling and longed for human connection. You forget how important something like that is. Hope for a new life filled my heart, and I couldn't wait to begin.

Staying sober inside the proverbial "padded walls" was a cakewalk. I felt good after a few days and could hold down food. Attending group sessions was optional, so I took the easier route of staying in bed and watching TV. Honestly, my mind was far removed from that place. I felt physically better and had some great ideas brewing in my head. I remember thinking, "Man, this was all I needed to be removed from heroin to have a fighting chance." I really thought I was going to walk out of there with some self-awareness and never have to touch heroin again. Fourteen days and I am fixed. A 14-day fix.

Chapter Five

Damage: Lisa

"Sometimes we are just the collateral damage
In someone else's war against themselves."
Lauren Eden

Whenever you read about addiction, wherever you go to a meeting and whatever professional you speak to, "Addiction is a disease of the family" comes up sooner or later. I had heard it or read it so many times it became a platitude, used too often to be interesting or thoughtful. But the truth is, you're so busy dealing with the addict and your own stress that you lose sight of the ripple effect. It's much more than a ripple; it's more like a rogue wave, bigger than you realize and unpredictable, crashing down and wiping away everything in its path. I heard somewhere that a rogue wave close to shore is called a sneaker wave. Addiction is like that; it sneaks up on a family, and by the time you see it, the damage has already been done.

You will also come across lists of roles family members take on, like the enabler, the lost child, or the hero. Labels are a big thing in addiction treatment. During family programs at rehabs, it's not unusual to give everyone a label to wear around their neck for the duration of the program. It is determined by those running the program, usually after only one day. I get the point; the role you have taken on in the family often dictates how you react to each situation, how that prolongs the addiction, and what damage you do to yourself. They see the same patterns repeatedly; hence the outcome, based on your role, is predictable. If you become aware of your role, they believe you will be able to change your pattern and understand your part in the family dynamic that hurts, not helps the addict. There's some truth to it, but I always thought it was too pat, too superficial. If you believe the label, it is as if your reactions are predestined, so you give yourself permission to react the way you do. The entire family will deal with issues and situations they could never have imagined. One day something small will make you cry, and another day sit in stunned silence. Your skin gets thicker, and the unbelievable becomes your new normal. Your reactions change over time as you lower your expectations. You go from wanting him to show up to a family event to hoping he doesn't overdose and die without identification. You never know what happened to him. There's no label for that transformation.

During one of the more difficult times of my separation from Gerad's father, my divorce attorney told me, "If you really want to know someone's true character, divorce them." This rule rings true with family and friends when you are dealing with an addict. I was lucky to have those that encouraged me and rooted for Gerad. I had others that enabled the enabler, feeding into my guilt and inability to "just make it go away." They were full of, "How could he do that to his daughter?" "How could he do that to his family?" and "He needs to just stop." I slowly avoided them and rarely went into detail when asked how Gerad was doing. I understood it was a difficult subject and, for most of them, unfathomable. A simple reply of, "He's doing OK," was acceptable to them. Subject avoided. Let's move on to more pleasant things. I wanted to say, "If you really want to know, he went to jail again, the infection in his hand is worse because he keeps shooting up in the same place, he stole my mother's debit card and withdrew money, I can't find my favorite bracelet, and oh, he is homeless now too." Too much information. They were uncomfortable with the subject, and I began losing patience, explaining that addiction isn't a choice. Luckily the opposite was true of the friends who really understood how difficult this had all become. They genuinely cared and often reminded me of who Gerad was before. "I love that kid; he'll find his way through this." "Hang in there, Lisa, I can't imagine how hard this must be for you and Gerad." You knew you were safe to talk about it by how they asked the question. There was an easing into it, a gentle tone. "Have you heard from Gerad?" "How are you holding up?" Even so, I spared them the dirty details. I felt strongly that I had their support but didn't feel I had the right to expose them to just how dark the life of an addict and its effect on the family can be. It's something I wouldn't wish on anyone.

It was hard to listen to friends as they reveled in their children's accomplishments as adults. College graduation, new career opportunities, marriage, and children. I just wanted my son to stay alive long enough to reach treatment. I was long over the high hopes I had for his life and could no longer remember a time when those things were possible for him. I just wanted him to be sober and have a life, a small, happy life in which he could find contentment and love. Was that so much to ask?

One of my many cheerleaders was Missy. I had known her since our paths crossed when I worked at the University. We became fast friends. She was funny and unassuming and had a heart of gold. She and Gerad always laughed together, and she had a way of communicating with him that always put him at ease. Missy was there for me in the darkest days of my divorce, and she would be there for me in some of the most difficult times with Gerad. When I first found out that Gerad was living on the streets, I called Missy for moral support. I told her I was thinking of going and looking for him. There was never any judgment from her, so I could tell her anything. There had just been an article in the paper about a homeless man living under a bridge who developed frostbite on his feet. He had refused medical care because he didn't have a way to pay for it. They had to amputate his feet. I was alone that weekend and concerned about poking around under bridges by myself. Without hesitation, she said she would grab her dogs and begin looking. It was one of those moments in life where you truly feel loved, despite the circumstances. Sometimes you must go to the darkest places to find those moments. When I had to go to Gerad's first court appearance, Missy immediately volunteered to take the trip with me. I picked her up at 5 am and began the trek to Elko. We laughed and reminisced about Gerad. It was good for my soul.

Cheerleader number two was Heidi. Although I hadn't known her as long, and she didn't know Gerad long before his addiction, she never wavered in her support. She had been with me the night of his motorcycle accident and drove me to the hospital. You could say she was there from the beginning through to the end of this nightmare. We often met for coffee, and she always asked for updates. She asked good questions and gently pushed me to stay strong. She was empathetic and caring and checked in with me regularly without being pushy. She cheered every small victory and cursed every setback. I knew she would be there in a split second if I needed her. We often traveled together, and she remained flexible, knowing there were times I couldn't leave. She was understanding and empathetic. She was a rock.

And then there is the person that just knows; without saying a word, they know the pain that sends you to the dark places. For me, that person was Cheryl. She had experienced the loss I was most afraid of, the loss of a child. She knew what it felt like not to be able to save them, no matter how hard you tried. I felt loved and supported just by being around her.

The dynamic is different when it's inside your family. Most of them lived away from me during this time. My oldest son was stationed at Fort Hood in Texas; my sister lived in Ohio, and my brother in San Francisco. Distance didn't deter any of them from encouragement and prayers. My Aunt had dealt with addiction through an alcoholic ex-husband and her youngest daughter. She checked in regularly through social media and texts. Each meant the world to me. My sister cried with me and laughed with me. Her support for Gerad was never shaken, and even though she lived far away, her love and support were invaluable. She never judged, just listened. In town and at home were my youngest son, my mother, and my husband. Gerad's father was also in town but was only peripherally involved. I'm not sure if he realized how bad things were with Gerad or if he did and stayed away, avoiding the tough stuff. Gerad occasionally contacted him for money, but they saw each other rarely. My youngest son took Gerad's addiction very hard. He had looked up to him. When Gerad first left our house after his first relapse, Alec wanted to get a group of friends and go find him. When we found out Gerad was homeless, his reaction was the same. In his eyes, Gerad's fall was mighty and incomprehensible. He thought Gerad could do anything. Both of his brothers' fear and empathy turned to anger toward the entire situation and their inability to fix it.

With my mother, it was complicated. She took Gerad in on occasion when I wouldn't let him come to my house. She inexhaustibly helped me contact detox centers and rehabs and took him to countless assessments. She went to one of his court hearings when I had to be out of town and to interviews to be considered for a rehab bed. He stole from her and took her car without permission, but he also sat with her and listened to her talk for hours. He would watch TV with her and keep her company. She would meet him in different places and buy him food. When she was in the hospital, he would walk to see her and stay in her room in the skilled nursing facility while she recuperated. Cynical people said he was just looking for a place to stay and food to eat, but I still believe he was genuinely worried about her. My mom has a very soft heart, and I would tell her not to give him money or food. She vehemently disagreed. Toward the end, when she asked where Gerad was, I told her he was living on the streets. She chastised me for allowing that to happen. "You can't just leave him on the streets," she told me emphatically. "Mom, it's the hardest thing I've ever done, but if we don't stop supporting him, he'll never be ready to get clean." She

71

had said the same thing to me about jail. There were times I felt like I was barely keeping it together, especially when I had to tell Gerad I wouldn't help him, and these statements hit hard. I know she meant well, and she truly cared about Gerad, but like so many people taking care of an addict, what you need to do is the opposite of what you think you should do. If there was an instruction manual we all received with our newborn babies, and it had a chapter on addiction, it would have one sentence: forget everything you just learned. No one comes equipped to deal with it. You can literally love them to death.

Sometimes it takes a complete stranger to let you know you are already on that path. I had the mother of an addict track me down at work looking for Gerad. I recognized her son's name when she mentioned it. Gerad had briefly introduced me to him right before he had to leave our house again the week before. When Gerad stayed with us, I was adamant that he couldn't bring people to our home. A few months earlier, a house down the street was broken into in broad daylight by the friend of their addict son looking for drugs the son had taken. I was often home alone since my husband traveled for his job, and I couldn't risk his circle of addicts and dealers knowing where we lived. But Gerad always picked up the stray cats and the down-and-outs; this guy had been accosted outside a coffee place, so Gerad had brought him back to the house so he could clean up. He was shy and sweet but definitely using. As his mother sat down across from my desk, she asked me where Gerad was because she needed to find him. I explained that I hadn't seen Gerad in a week or so and had no idea where she could find him. She told me her son had called her from jail the day before, and when she asked what happened to his stepfather's motorcycle he had been riding, he told her Gerad loaded it into his truck, and that was the last he'd seen of it. She had tracked me down through social media and had been running around town fixing the mess he had left in his wake. I instantly saw myself in her. I smiled slightly and told her, "Gerad doesn't have the motorcycle. He doesn't have a truck, and even if he did, it wouldn't matter because he can't use his right arm. There's no way he could load a motorcycle into anything. Your son sold or traded the motorcycle for drugs." She began to cry. I gently told her I understood what she was trying to do, but my best advice was to stop. Stop running around trying to make everything OK because it's not OK. I could tell she wasn't listening and was on the same mission I had been on. I tried a different approach, "Isn't it funny, even from jail, he wants you to believe in him, believe he is a good person, and hear you still love him." She paused, sat up straight, wiped her eyes, and left. I knew it would be a long time before she reached the point where she could finally save them both. I hoped I was getting closer to that place.

In many ways, the most damage was directed at my husband, Gerad's stepfather. We found out Gerad was an addict just a few months shy of our two-year anniversary. He had kids considerably younger than mine, and they were with us every other week. He had to walk a tightrope between supporting me and protecting his kids. Not an easy task. Before the worst of his addiction, Gerad and Barry got along. It was hard on all my boys to bring another man into our lives. I had been married to their father for 28 years, and it had been a rocky divorce, but Gerad made the best of it. Eventually, Gerad saw Barry as a roadblock to manipulating me. Understandably their relationship went downhill as Gerad's addiction raged on.

Barry was right there for me after Gerad's accident, and his insurance is the reason we were able to get Gerad the surgery that would restore much of the use of his arm and hand. When I brought Gerad to our home after first finding out about the heroin, Barry and my youngest son went back to Gerad's house with a gun to keep the squatters from coming back. The young couple had jimmied a window and locked the door to the room they had been sleeping in so they could continue to have access. The girl was pregnant. Gerad had brought unwanted guests to the house several times, and Barry worried others would come looking for drugs or worse for Gerad. Barry slept with a gun, yet he allowed me to bring Gerad back over and over. Barry found a small pack of meth in our front courtyard, needles in various places, and remnants of balloons, but he still gave in to my requests and let him come back. He was able to see Gerad through different eyes than the eyes of his mother. He warned me that Gerad did absolutely nothing when I left the house and pushed me to keep him active and occupied. While serving his son's breakfast one morning, a girl walked into our house and said Gerad told her to come over and get breakfast. We didn't even know someone was with him. He had to ask who she was and tell her to leave. Through it all, I defended Gerad. I wanted him to understand who Gerad was before all this happened. I wanted him to know there was still good in Gerad, and if I could just keep him alive long enough, I knew he would get fed up and get clean. We went to counseling to try and lower the pressure we both felt. I felt ashamed and guilty for bringing Barry into the mess that was our lives. He saw the worst of it all and was still stuck by my side. He rooted for Gerad even after he stole from him and agreed to pay for rehab even after previous attempts to get clean failed. He knew I would never give up on Gerad and watched the process age me before his eyes. I learned more about love and grace from him than anyone at any time in my life.

The biggest victim was Gerad's daughter. His brothers did an amazing job with her, and I've never been prouder of them. I talked about him all the time to her, hoping to keep him in her thoughts. I bought presents for birthdays, Christmas and Easter I claimed were from her daddy. I even got him to appear a few times, shoving the gift in his hand so he could give it to her. I made excuses for why he wasn't around and mentioned everything she did that reminded me of him. When he did come home, I would bring her up to see him. I always thought a sense of normalcy and seeing his daughter would snap him out of it. That was before I understood that his thoughts were no longer his own. I bought them paint sets to do together and pads to draw on. He would color with her for hours but eventually would lie on the couch, glued to his phone as she played on her own. He made it to her kindergarten graduation and the first day of elementary school with my coaxing. He saw her ride her first bike with training wheels and watched as my husband ran her up and down the street, learning to ride without them. He made it to a few family birthday dinners she attended and most holiday dinners. He missed birthdays and Easter egg hunts, trick-or-treating, and her first father-daughter dance. He had always been the one to take her trick-or-treating and called me from jail the first time he would miss it, choked up, but it wasn't enough to make him stop. She grew tall and lovely without him. Her interests grew and changed from gymnastics to dance, to making potions from what she found outside to creating a book of her shoe designs. He should have been there when she wanted to learn to skateboard. Gerad excelled at it, and it would have been nice for him to pass those skills on to her, along with snowboarding and playing the guitar. She did pick up his artistic side and spent many hours at my kitchen table drawing. Occasionally, Gerad would paint her pictures, and she would hang them in her room. Her walls were full of the art he had made while at university, but his absence was deafening. They say kids are resilient, and I hoped she didn't notice, but she surprised us all when she had her chance to express her fear and sadness. We were stunned at how much she had been affected. Another casualty of addiction.

Chapter Five

Damage: Gerad

"Woke up next to last,
Torn apart by my past.
Run away from my pain,
But I guess it's here to stay.
'cause I don't live to be,
Whatever you think of me."
Think of Me, lyrics by Gerad Davis

There's a point on this journey where you accept that you are a bad person. That's what I believed for a long time. Before I knew about the disease of addiction, I really thought I was a terrible person lacking the moral and philosophical compass of ordinary people. I would have the best intentions to do right by my family, but my actions never followed through. I couldn't stick to the plan, ever. I didn't realize the pain I was causing until I surfaced with a sober mind. It didn't seem real when I heard the stories of the pain and suffering my family went through. It was like some dark fairytale with no happy ending. I obviously never wanted that for any of them. I later learned that I didn't have a choice in the matter. Any sane person would never choose to inflict pain on their family the way that I did for years. As you get further and further down the rabbit hole, everyone around you detaches. They sever you like an unsavable limb; it's too painful to keep fighting. My family was the exception.

My selfishness continued when I got sober and made amends to them. I expected everyone to cheer for me and welcome me back with open arms. More than anything, I expected them to trust me immediately. I dug out their hearts for years like a mineral mine. I slowly dug further and further down and created multiple levels of deception until it turned into this unimaginable crater. It took years to create that hole, and I wanted it filled up with love and happiness. I was standing at the top of this crater with a shovel, throwing in scoops of dirt, and wanting them to see the effort and applaud me for it. The truth is, it took me years to dig it out, and it was going to take years to put it all back.

If you believe other people will keep you sober, you are setting yourself up for failure. If that were true, I would have stayed sober for Tatum. She was such an easy kid that showed nothing but love for me, even through my darkest moments. The first few years of her life, we were inseparable. I couldn't comprehend the damage I was doing. She was only two years old when I had my accident. It was difficult to care for her during that time. Once the opiates started, the unfavorable people began to trickle into my life. She was around a lot of drug use as my house became a revolving door for the lost souls trying to forget their pain. My mom would question me about the people I had over, and she told me she had a premonition that something bad would happen to Tatum. Thankfully, it never came true. The scary part was that idea didn't bother me as much as it would have if I had been sober. If I had been really concerned about her safety, I would have stopped. I was entitled to the point where I wanted all the best moments without the responsibility of the difficult ones. I expected my mom to take care of her, and she did when I asked. My attitude shifted to this victim mentality, where I expected everyone to feel sorry for me and take care of me. I became this ungrateful leech.

There were good memories during that time too. I created a lot of artwork with Tatum. I admired the kid's ability to create without filters. There was never any doubt when she would spew colors all over a blank canvas. There was so much confidence in her eyes and enough curiosity to carry us both. She settled my crazy mind during those times. I wanted her to be proud of me. I wanted my whole family to be proud of me, but they all fell victim to my ego and pride. Our relationship was sparse after I left the house that she was raised in. The only reason I stayed for as long as I did was because my grandmother owned the house. When my mom figured out what was going on, she put the whole situation to a stop with the help of my stepdad. It wasn't a safe environment anymore, and at the time, I couldn't see why it was such a big deal. I didn't think I had a problem, even though the evidence showed that things were going downhill fast. I rented my rooms out for drugs and even gave up my own bed if it meant I would stay high for another day. Once I let them in, it was damn near impossible to get rid of them. I didn't have the confidence to stand up to anyone, so even if I didn't like a situation, I would rather accept it than change it. Losing that house was the beginning of a long road of struggle and uncertainty.

While my mom was catching on to my behaviors and learning how to deal with them, my grandmother had a different philosophy. She had the kind of love that kills an addict, the one that most parents adapt when their child is born. Nanny wanted the best for me and thought I should never be on the street or go hungry. Selfishly, I used that against her when I had nowhere else to go. I stayed at her house after the first time I went to detox and promised everyone that I would do better. I loved spending time with her and watching shows, but I had this hunger that I couldn't ignore. Imagine starving and choosing not to eat. That's what the itch of heroin felt like. Things were good for about a week before I started rifling through her medicine cabinet. When I used everything I could find, I started taking her car at night and stealing her debit card to score heroin. My mom managed her bank accounts and caught on quickly. I blatantly kept doing it because I knew my grandmother wasn't a confrontational person. When she finally asked me about her debit card, I made a huge scene and walked out of her house with nowhere to go. I remember that night well because I walked all the way to downtown Reno in the middle of the night. I took whatever I could find from her garage and knew where I could go to trade it for a couple of balloons. I trudged the road until it was morning before I finally made it to my destination. I was willing to go to any length to get my next fix. The funny part was the guy I was looking for moved motels, and I ended up pawning the random tools and going somewhere else.

I had faith in the dumbest things. My family relationships became very transactional. I would only stick around if my needs were met. I would vanish in the blink of an eye if any kind of altercation came up. I only kept in contact with people that would help me. I didn't talk to either of my brothers much during this time. I would see them at the occasional holiday event, but all our talks were very superficial. I found out later how much of an impact I had on both of their lives.

My stepdad got the worst treatment of everyone. He married my mom when I was older, so it took me a long time to give him the respect he deserved. I was so caught up in the "I don't need another dad" mentality that I failed to see the good that he provided for the family. When things started to get bad, I would steal from him every chance I got. I remember buying them a safe for Christmas one year, and I knew the combination. I later broke into it to steal his Rolex watch. I would take cash out of his wallet if he left it lying around and always looked through his things. The most brazen thing I stole was the diamond tennis bracelet he got for my mom on Christmas. I remember being especially dope sick that morning when we were unwrapping gifts. When I saw my mom place it on the counter to take a shower, I snatched it without hesitation. She didn't even have it for an hour before I took it to a jeweler and sold it for a measly $250. I then found out that he had paid $5,000 for that bracelet. Later I got the opportunity to pay him back for it. It felt good to make that right, even though I basically got pennies for it. When I confessed to it, I found out that my mom thought she had lost it and felt guilty. Those were things that I took for granted.

It was hard to account for all the confusion and bullshit I caused to those closest to me. I put his boys in danger by being sneaky and bringing people around the house without them knowing. Barry was smart and hyper-aware of what was going on and made it very difficult for me to get what I wanted. I resented him for it at the time, but it's hard to say where I would be without his cutthroat accountability. He was never scared to confront me and call me on my shit, but he was also always there to take me to rehab, show up at my court cases or force me to get up off my ass when I was sicker than a dog. What I used to qualify as borderline abuse, I now see as genuine caring. The impact of those moments showed me how he was just as much of a cheerleader for me as my mom. He never mentioned how much he paid for treatments, detox, or fixing up my car. He found countless needles, used spoons, and drugs around his house, but he never held any of that over my head. I respect the humility that was required when I was a wrecking ball in his life. If he was the only person I had in my life, I would have gotten sober way sooner than I did. Every addict or alcoholic needs a Barry in their life. The right amount of tough love and support.

The hardest lesson for me to learn was that life goes on. Whether you go to jail, end up homeless on the streets, or die, life around you continues. I saw my daughter grow up in glimpses, and I hated myself for it. She became brighter and taller without me, so I came to terms with the fact that she didn't need me to survive. I wanted to get sober for her. I wanted her to be a big enough reason for me to set things right and get out of my misery. That's not how it works though; I know because I tried for years to do it for her. The good part is that I had a family that took great care of her and helped her stay connected to me when I was disconnected, like a telephone left off the hook for too long. My mom and brothers did a lot of heavy lifting that went unnoticed for a long time. I remember visiting home for Christmas when I was about two years sober. I was so excited to be involved and present that I helped my mom prepare food and set up the festivities. I became judgmental toward my brothers because they weren't helping to the same extent as I was. I told my mom about the anger I felt. She stopped me dead in my tracks by saying, "Gerad, Ryan and Alec have always taken care of Tatum, especially around the holidays. You haven't been around much in the past few years. Show them some grace." That statement smacked my ego down as I saw the importance of what they were doing behind the scenes.

I didn't have much direct contact with my brothers when I was using, but I kept unveiling the things that they did when I wasn't around. They tirelessly helped keep the ship afloat. Both went out looking for me on several occasions and kept it to themselves about how scared they were and how hopeless they felt. They never called me names or yelled at me. There are so many moving parts in a family dynamic it's painful to process when the fog lifts. I learned a lot about what goes unsaid between people in your life. It's tragic to think about all the pain that others feel that they keep close to their heart. Loving an addict is no easy task. I was grateful when I got to discuss my mistakes with them. Each opened up to me about the pain they felt. I learned about so many things I did to harm them. So, it begs the question, can the suffering be helped by asking them directly how they feel? I don't want any more casualties in my story, lost voices with no one to tell. This disease affects the whole family, everyone needs help, and no one wants to ask for it.

Chapter Six

Backsliding: Lisa

"The disease of addiction is a chronic,
devious bitch just waiting for you to slip up."
D.C. Hayden

I was told, very late in the game, that relapse is a normal part of recovery, but nothing about it feels normal. I truly believed that once Gerad stopped using, he would stop using. He would be thankful to be out of the drug's grip and appreciate how much better life could be sober. Simple. For the first few days after the withdrawals stopped, and he came out of the fog, that was the case. I heard it called "rehab high," where they feel grateful, hopeful, and full of ideas for the future. Unfortunately, the problems he had just weeks before came back to haunt him, and the pull to escape was too strong. After witnessing two agonizing withdrawals, I learned my first lesson in the cycle of recovery and relapse: a "recovery" didn't start because they detoxed and got through withdrawals; it only cracked the door open. Recovery is making a choice to walk through that door, and it had to be theirs alone. When I wasn't relentlessly pursuing getting him into rehab, I would try creating a goal: going back to school or pursuing a new career path. I even asked him where he'd like to travel when he got sober, promising him a trip to the destination of his choice. New York, it was always New York. I couldn't fathom the power of that tug to go right back down the dark tunnel instead of moving toward the light, no matter how many times I witnessed it.

Somewhere around attempt five, I understood he was only claiming he wanted to get clean when he had run out of options and only going to detox because I was relentless in my insistence. I didn't know it at the time, but my laser focus on pushing him into treatment without giving him a choice was the cause of so many temporary bouts of sobriety. Without a long-term plan for actual recovery and his buy-in, it was doomed to fail. I would become fixated on getting him to a safe place, excited he was willing to try and believed I could figure out the next steps once the crisis passed. Treatment centers were still impossible to get into, and the few outpatient treatments were ineffective. Sometimes he made it for a month, sometimes a couple of weeks, and more often than not, only days. All I was doing was further convincing him that trying to get sober was a pipe dream, and worse, I realized it was my dream, not his.

During one of his sober times, he told me, "Mom, I'm scared all the time." It was one of the few things I could relate to since I seemed to be living in a constant state of fear. Nonetheless, I was surprised to hear him say it. Gerad had seemed to gain so much confidence after high school. He didn't just snowboard; he had to do extreme snowboarding. He would DJ at parties and leaned to spin fire entertaining his large circle of friends. But somewhere in there was still the sweet, sensitive boy I knew.

When he was a young boy, any loud noise sent him sprinting to get away. Although we learned to expect the reaction at certain events, I thought continuing to expose him would help him be less fearful. His dad was a college football coach, and after a touchdown, they would fire a cannon, so I usually didn't take him to the games. By the end of one season, when Gerad was four, I thought I would try. We parked, made our way to the stands and began searching for our seats. Before we could sit down, the cannon fired. I had prepared a plan to distract Gerad if a touchdown happened, but this was unexpected. Those short, little four-year-old legs sent Gerad sprinting toward the parking lot. No warning scream, no look of terror that I could react to, just a blonde blur running as fast as he could to get away from that noise. As usual, I took off after him, partly amazed at just how fast he could run and partly terrified he would get hit by a car in the parking lot. These mad dashes had become a regular occurrence. I know it wasn't loud noises he was trying to run away from now, but the fear was just as real. "Everyone's scared, honey, but we have to find our way." When and how that would happen seemed very far away.

After having tried and failed with the psychiatrist and Suboxone in his first attempt to get clean, we next tried the methadone clinic. After coming home thin, pale, and as sick as I had ever seen him, he was the one to bring it up. Since it was his idea, I was hoping he would commit to making it work. His withdrawal started within hours of his coming home, and the symptoms were immediately brutal. On top of his poor condition, the whites of his eyes were yellow, and I was certain he had contracted Hepatitis. He only had to endure it until the next morning when the clinic opened. When I called the Life Change Center, they explained the process. He would be evaluated, and if he qualified for this treatment, he would get a medical exam and blood work. They also required attendance at outpatient group therapy sessions. The program was built around accountability and trust, two things addicts lack. Initially, you had to come in every day to get your dose. Eventually, you could graduate to once a week and so forth. It would mean a commitment on my part to get him there every day, with no end in sight. It was impossible to think about what that would mean long-term, but then I wasn't thinking of that, only that we would be lucky to be in this for the long run.

We made the drive to Sparks and pulled up to a one-story brick building. There wasn't anything that distinguished the building from those around it. I'm sure people drove by it every day with no clue of what was happening inside. The waiting room was brightly lit with fluorescent lights and very sterile with beige chairs, walls, floors, beige everything. No frills, no mess, and no fuss. When I had called the day before, I was told intake was between 6 am and 7 am. They only did so many intakes per day, and it was on a first come, first served basis. There were two counters encased in very thick glass, one marked intake and the other marked medication. We had arrived right at 6 am, and a line was already forming at the desk to check in for medication. I went to the intake counter to get the paperwork and sat down with Gerad, but not before noticing the colorful bowl of candy with a handwritten sign: "One piece per child." Did people really bring their children here?

Gerad was having trouble sitting up and staying still. His eyes were half closed, and his lips were pulled tight. He looked dehydrated, with chapped lips and sunken cheeks. We had gotten this far. I just needed him to hang on a bit longer. This was the sickest I had ever seen him. I had no idea how long the wait would be, and when he occasionally opened his eyes, he looked toward the door as if weighing his options to stay or go. The only reason he stayed was he was just too damn sick to move.

After forty-five minutes, his name was called, and we were escorted into a small room with a round table. The usual set of questions about his drug use and medical history were methodically gone through, notes taken, and then the evaluator took one last look at his notes and looked up, concluding that he would qualify for treatment. I expressed my concern that he might have Hepatitis, and they assured me he would receive a thorough exam with labs. Gerad followed the evaluator to an exam room. I went back to the waiting room. As I looked up, I noticed the line at the dose counter was even longer. I was shocked to see people in scrubs, high school coaching shirts, men in ties, and women in suits waiting to get their dose before heading to work. I remember shaking my head at my own biases of what an addict should be. It certainly wasn't my sons' math teacher or the guy that sold me my car insurance. I had been living in a bubble of many layers, and another layer had just burst.

When his exam was complete, Gerad was escorted into the waiting room, and we were told they would call us with his lab results in a few days. He was given a small dose of methadone. A treatment counselor explained that Gerad's dose would slowly be increased until his withdrawal symptoms and cravings stopped. There was no way to know how long that would take. He was instructed to bring a small locking case from now on to place his dose in, and so we began the routine of waking early, driving to the center, and waiting. Waiting for him to start feeling "normal," waiting for his symptoms to subside, and waiting to see if this time worked.

Gerad was required to attend group therapy to continue to receive the methadone and gravitated to the group leader John, a recovering addict. His story resonated with Gerad, and he trusted him. He would often quote John or tell me a piece of John's story he'd shared with the group.

Lesson two: only another addict can understand what you are asking of someone seeking recovery. They understand all the dark places the addict has been. They are also the only ones that can call them on their crap when the addict believes they don't need a formal program and that they can do it on their own. A recovering addict is also the only person the addict will believe to see that a sober life is possible.

After surviving the first week, Gerad was eating better, and his bloodwork came back in good shape. I told him he had dodged another bullet, and we decided my dad was his guardian angel. Gerad seemed to like the idea. The clinic continued to increase his dose, and there were days he seemed like his old self, but his energy level was still low, which I attributed to exhaustion. At some point, he began sleeping a lot, getting headaches and nausea. It turned out the "cure" was worse than the drugs. Gerad began to complain that the methadone was making him sick. We talked to the nurse who administered the doses, and she said to stay the course. It was normal for your body to continue to adjust for the first month. He didn't make it that long.

Lesson three: don't ignore the signs. Giving pep talks, words of encouragement, and being at their beck and call doesn't work.

87

Gerad began keeping to himself and barely getting out of bed. My husband told me that when I wasn't there, he never came out of his room. He began asking to go out for mundane errands when we were all busy and couldn't accompany him. It sounds so silly now, but I wanted to trust him. Manipulation only happened when he was using, right? So, when he was trying to get sober, I wanted him to believe I trusted and supported him. In reality, it was during these bouts to get clean when the manipulation was at its worst. When he was using, he didn't deny it, and our expectations were realistic. When he was "trying" to get clean, he wasn't trying at all. He just had to up the manipulation game to make me believe he really wanted to change his life. As he sat at my kitchen table one day, I could tell something was different. I asked him what was going on. He said he had gotten some Xanax from a friend to help deal with his anxiety. I didn't even know he had left the house. "Everything is fine, Mom." I was focused on the future, the possibility of this being over, and I had been played again. He left a few days later.

When he came home and agreed to detox, once again, I felt like I had learned from my mistakes. Upon admission to West Hills, they agreed to keep him for two weeks this time and enroll him in their intensive outpatient therapy program. Once again, no inpatient rehab beds were available in the 30,60- or 90-day treatment centers in Nevada. He would have to attend therapy sessions five days per week for four hours. His Medicaid would again cover his admission and the outpatient program. I visited him on every visitation day, standing around the lobby with all the other families, anxious to see progress. They would line us up outside the cafeteria while the patients were brought in and seated individually at a table. The cafeteria was as utilitarian as the rest of the building, with bars on the window to remind you this wasn't just any hospital. I would chat aimlessly about what was happening with the rest of the family as Gerad rested his head against his arm and stared at me through glassy eyes. He said detox was tough, but they gave him Valium, which helped with the symptoms. An orderly had befriended him and told Gerad he reminded him of his son. Gerad liked their talks, and it seemed to be a bright spot for him. He also liked the doctor that checked in on him daily. We were allowed to drop off a few things, the most important for him being cigarettes. Although I hated smoking, it seemed so harmless compared to what else he had put in his body.

Two weeks passed quickly, and I went to pick him up. He was upbeat and happy to be leaving. He had made a friend, Will, and was looking forward to what came next. His therapy group started the next day, and on day two, the staff approached him and told him there was a problem with his Medicaid and that he would have to leave until he straightened it out. He came home, and we immediately got on the phone to try and find out what was happening. We were told it could be fixed, but the system wouldn't show him as covered for at least a week. He assured me it was fine, but I knew this hiccup was a problem. I watched him like a hawk, but he was free to roam at night. I called West Hills daily, and when I finally got confirmation that he could come back, I dropped him off at his session, but as I drove away, something told me to look back. As I rounded the corner to turn onto the main road, I saw Gerad and a girl take off out the front door and hop into a car. Although I doubted he was clean, I knew it would break his daughter's heart if he missed her birthday. He had been working on a gift for her, so when I asked him to go with me to pick up my gift, he said he wanted to stay and finish it. An hour later, I came home to find him passed out on her bed and a needle on the floor.

Lesson four: everything works against you; the lack of rehab beds, insurance glitches, and most importantly, time. If you are lucky enough to get them into detox, they must immediately go to treatment, and then the fight begins to convince them to stay the course. That is the hardest part. One glitch, and they're gone.

You learn to be prepared in case an opportunity arises to get an addict into treatment. I searched the internet and researched all the programs in our area, hoping to find the magic bullet that would open the door. Several of the places did contact me when they had a bed available, but it was always when Gerad was MIA. I talked to a friend who was dating a Board member of a program called Step 1. It was a treatment program mainly for men coming out of jail, but they did have a couple of beds for others. When a detective called looking for Gerad on an outstanding warrant, I told them where they could probably find him and asked if he would go to jail. I explained that he was an addict and that I could get him into Step 1 if he was coming from jail. I asked him to notify me if they found him, and I would call the program. I told the detective, "This is your chance to save his life." I don't think it moved him, and I'm positive it was not the conversation he had expected, but I never expected to help the police find my son and ask them to put him in jail. They did find him, and they did take him to jail. I even got a call from a social worker. It was a Friday, and she explained she wasn't on duty that weekend but would leave a note asking that he not be released until they called me. I didn't hear from anyone Monday morning, so I called and was told he had been released. Another failure.

Lesson five: you will continue to lower the bar. You will do things you never thought you would do to save your child.

Out of the blue, Gerad called one day and told me his friend was getting a Suboxone prescription from a psychiatrist in town that worked with West Hills hospital. Gerad wanted to try once again. I called and confirmed the clinic would take Medicaid and made an appointment. He had conveniently opened his office across the street from the detox facility, and judging from the packed waiting room, he had picked the right spot. After an hour's wait, we were called into his office and sat across a massive desk from him in a room full of books and mismatched furniture. There was no medical exam and few health questions. This guy was checking the boxes to legally prescribe Suboxone and nothing more. Gerad was told he would have to come back into the office to get his prescriptions. That was it. No therapy, no sessions, just show up.

Lesson six: there is no shortage of people that are willing to make money off your loved one's addiction.

Gerad would drift in and out of our lives. Any contact had an ask attached, food, money, or a hotel room for the night. Once, I met him in the parking lot of a grocery store after he called for my help. As I approached his car, I could see he was passed out behind the wheel. My heart felt like it was going to beat out of my chest as I tapped on the window, wondering if this was it, the overdose I had feared. He stirred, asked if I would help him with gas, and as soon as his tank was filled, he drove off and disappeared again. Twice he called so shaken I thought it would shake him right into recovery; he had revived his best friend when he overdosed. I picked him up and we drove around, talking about how he was done and he wanted to plan for the future. He said he had been walking around all night thinking about how to change his life. During this time, he always looked terrible with a scraggly beard, baggy clothes, long, greasy hair, and smelled of sweat, dirt, and too much time in the same clothes. As usual, I just smiled and said hello. I felt lucky to have him in front of me and just listened, never mentioning anything I thought would agitate him. I would drop him off where I had picked him up, with assurances he would let me know when to come to get him. Then, like a ghost, he would disappear.

Because I had vowed not to bring him back to the house again, he was homeless, so I would sometimes get him a room for the night or even a couple of days. I was even delusional enough to take him to look at apartments, still not understanding that the drug was the most important thing in his life, not food, not shelter, and not even his life. No question he would have allowed me to pay for it, but luckily one look at him by the apartment manager, and he would be turned down. When he still had a car, he would sleep in it, but one night he parked in the wrong spot, and the car got towed. By the time he told me about it, the impound wanted over $7,000 to claim it. The car wasn't worth that much. With the help of an attorney friend, they agreed to take the title to the car instead.

I couldn't imagine leaving him homeless. Up to this point, he had always found a place to crash even though that place, and the people involved, remained a revolving door. In my infinite wisdom, I found the cheapest, tiniest, no-lease, furnished apartment in downtown Reno and put him up there for months. It kept him off the street, and apparently, several others he let stay. He eventually kicked out his best friend, who had no means to contribute to food or drugs, but he had a girl he had been with for over a year, and they stayed put, occasionally allowing someone with something to contribute to hang out. The owners of the building didn't seem to mind. The building was full of addicts and drifters, and if you paid the rent, no one questioned your comings and goings.

Lesson seven: the hardest lesson, you cannot support an addict in any way if you want them to conclude that getting sober was their only choice. There would be many rock bottoms, and many near-death experiences, to the point you couldn't fathom what rock bottom would be. It doesn't happen quickly, and things get much worse than you could imagine, but it does happen. I finally stopped paying the rent, and he soon moved to the streets. Giving him shelter only made it easier to stay an addict.

A month later, his girlfriend was picked up by the police on an outstanding warrant as they walked down the street. The walls were starting to close in on him, and he was running out of options. The girlfriend had been adept at shoplifting and had a family that would sometimes help her out. Almost all addicts are wanted for something, usually associated with petty theft, possession, vagrancy, etc. From jail, she was put into a program, and Gerad never saw her again. In a 24-hour city, there are often places addicts can go inside, charge their phones, use the bathroom, and get warm. Gerad's go-to spot installed facial recognition that could identify anyone with a warrant or previous arrests and convictions. Gerad was quickly banned. He made it six months alone. As winter was approaching, he was sleeping under a highway overpass. I got the call a week before Thanksgiving in 2016.

Chapter Six

Backsliding: Gerad

"I guess my biggest problem is
that I find it easier to relapse
than to carry through."
S.A. Hawks

Relapse is expected when you never want to be sober in the first place; it's just a normal part of this rollercoaster ride. It took me a long time to figure out why I kept going back to heroin every time I would sober up. The withdraws were miserable but quickly forgotten. I couldn't recall the suffering each time I started. I knew logically that this life was not sustainable, and the consequences were obvious. I had to experience every option out there before it would ever make any real difference in my life. I met many heroin users that were doing methadone. I thought life would be more manageable if I tried it out. What they don't tell you is that these clinics want you to be dependent on them for a long time. They make money by having a quota of patients. Most clinics will increase your dosage to the point where it would be impossible to stop. Another thing they fail to mention is that withdrawal from methadone can last twice as long as withdrawal from street heroin. This system is set up to make money, not heal people that are struggling to survive.

With that being said, when I went to the clinic, it was the first time I was treated like a human being since becoming an addict. They had mandatory group therapy sessions, and I felt connected to other people that had endured the same agony that I had. This was my first glimpse at what would later become my lifeline to staying sober. Addicts helping other addicts to find hope in this world and show them how they did it. The guy running it said something that has stuck with me to this day: "Your family and friends will want the old you back, but that person is long gone. You must embrace the new version of yourself from this point on." I wanted the old me back too, but I realized at that moment how unrealistic that idea was. It was one more sobering reality of my addiction. I wanted so badly to be "normal."

Methadone didn't work for several reasons. When I took the dose in the morning, I felt lethargic and nauseous all day and really didn't get any motivation. The second thing I realized is it wasn't just the heroin I was addicted to but the lifestyle as well. I welcomed the chaos of figuring out how I was going to score for the day. I hung out with people that were on my level, so there was never any judgment. I missed fitting into my surroundings and not having to act like I was something that I wasn't. It became more and more challenging to be around family as things spiraled out of control. I had to put on a good face to talk to the people that loved me the most. The shame and guilt were hard for me to understand at that time. I just know that I was so uncomfortable not being able to recreate the old me for my family.

I went through the motions for as long as I could. I was barely hanging on every time I called my mom to get help. I wanted to keep using the way I had been without all the consequences that came with it. I had massive trauma that I failed to acknowledge. I believed deep down that I was going to die this way. The detoxes and other programs became more and more clinical, and I knew that they weren't going to help me in the long run. They were good for acute withdrawal symptoms, but there was never any change in my spiritual wellbeing. I was broken inside for years and kept putting bandages on it, hoping it would go away like a cut or bruise. I had to find what I was recovering from before I could start recovery. And that was a process I extremely underestimated.

I had a childlike ignorance of the life-and-death consequences of what I was doing. It was a gloomy cloud that always filled the room. I guess I didn't notice because of how dark things had become. There were countless times that my friends or girlfriends would overdose right in front of me, and I would have to smack the life into them. I was coming home in the early morning one day after walking the streets all night from casino to casino with my drug dealer. We went up to my room in an old apartment building in downtown Reno. My mom was paying the rent for this place out of sheer guilt, I'm sure. She didn't want me to be on the streets. Shit, I didn't want to be on the streets either. We exited the elevator and headed down the hall. I remember getting an eerie feeling, but I also had been up for several days at that point. It's hard to tell what's real when you lack sleep. I went to enter my room, and the door was locked. I knew my friend was in there because we had left him there hours before. He refused to go out with us, so I left him my key and told him we would be back. I pounded on the door, but there was no answer. Mind you, this was a 400-square-foot place, so it was hard not to hear when someone was banging on the door. I was confused and decided to call him. As soon as I dialed the phone, I could hear the cheesy ringtone from inside the room. I pounded on the door again, and still, no answer. I thought to myself, "Shit, he must be passed out."

My dealer friend and I decided to find a discrete place and smoke some meth while we waited for him to wake up. We weren't trying hard to hide what we were doing. We literally took a few turns down random hallways and set up camp. I think I got to a point where I just didn't give a shit who saw me doing whatever. During this sidebar, I continued to call my friend. I could hear the faint ringtone through the paper-thin walls of the building. I wish I could say that it dawned on me right away that he overdosed, but it didn't register, for at least 30 minutes, maybe an hour? Who the fuck knows. When it finally clicked, it hit me like a freight train.

"Wasn't Jake getting a bunch of Xanax last night?" My dealer asked.

I remembered he was known for taking way too many Xanax at one time.

"OH MY GOD, what if he is dead in my place!?" I said.

Now, a normal person who was sober and of sound mind would immediately call 911, but I was far from that garden state. I weighed my options with the drug dealer, who generally aren't known for giving the best advice.

"We should leave immediately," he said. "If he's dead, YOU will be in deep shit."

To be honest, I heavily considered running away and never looking back. I almost left my best friend at the time to die alone. This was a moment that gave me hope that I still had a soul. I decided to stay and called 911. That call took me off guard. The man who answered sounded apathetic and cold. He questioned the severity of the situation, and I was instantly annoyed.

"Are you sure he is locked in the room?"

"Yes!" I yelled.

"Does he have a history of drug use?"

"What the hell does that matter? He is unresponsive and has drugs in the room!"

He sighed and said, "Someone will be there shortly."

When any situation happens, it only feels like it's happening to you. I'm sure the dispatcher had several overdoses in a night, but it felt like a personal attack. After I made the call, I looked around for my dealer, who had pulled a Houdini and vanished into thin air. Typical behavior, every man for himself. I waited eagerly by my door for help. Seconds turned to minutes. I paced vigorously back and forth down the hall, and finally, the fire department arrived. A group of six men approached my door and instantly started asking questions. "How long has he been in there?" "Where have you been all night?" "What drugs is he using?" It's hard to remember what I said to them. I know I told them I was working a graveyard shift at a local casino. I always had this urge to lie to everyone in any situation. My pride told me I needed to look a certain way. I lost myself a long time ago.

A few crowded around my door as the questions continued. I heard one guy, who I assumed was the man in charge, tell a rookie to kick the door down. The rookie, brimming with excitement, stood in front of the door and kicked as hard he could but fell flat on his ass. I saw this in movies and assumed you always kicked a door in, facing it and kicking forward. The veteran laughed and helped the rookie off the floor and said, "Look, this isn't a TV show. You must stand with your back to the door and kick it like a donkey. You generate more force that way without hurting yourself." The veteran effortlessly did exactly what he explained and got the door open first try. I couldn't help but think to myself, is this a training exercise? You do know someone is dying on the other side of the door, don't you? The men filled the room and located Jake on the bed. He still wasn't responding, even after a freight train was coming through the door. I stood from the hallway looking in and could see drug paraphernalia all over the desk and floor. I was terrified of what that would mean for me. It was always about me in the end. The rookie leaned over my friend and yelled his name. As soon as he went to grab him, Jake shot up out of bed, shocked by his surroundings. He was so pale that his dark brown hair had turned blonde. It took him a few seconds to say anything, but he muttered, "I'm fine."

"Do you need medical attention?"

"No, I need to get the fuck out of here."

I will never regret my decision to call for help that day. This was one of those occurrences that scared me enough to rethink my current state. I had a conversation with my mom after that happened, and it was the first time I told her I didn't want to live the way I was living. It was a seed that was planted but would take a long time to sprout. Shortly after that, my mom stopped paying the rent and I was out on the street.

When you first become homeless, you constantly worry about how you must look to other people. A disgusting disgrace to society. Always dirty and smelling like a sunbaked garbage can. I would wear the same clothes for weeks on end, occasionally taking "bird baths" in the Truckee River. After a while, you become accustomed to the lifestyle, and the thought of what other people think is non-existent. I found comfort in resting by the river downtown because it was a lot cooler than the crackling asphalt and cement sidewalks. I was so exhausted from trudging around in the heat one summer afternoon that I quickly headed to my sanctuary. I made it to a public park by the river and sat down on the grass. It felt like there were a hundred families there that day, and it was impossible to ignore the exuberance, talking and laughing, like "normal" people. I was in a black hole of loneliness and despair. I was way past being out of place. I was an unnoticeable, a worm burrowed deep in the grass. I took this time to check on my abscessed hand. I unwrapped the old crusty gauze to inspect the golf ball-sized lump on my hand. I always hoped these things would magically evaporate, but this one was getting far worse than any I had experienced before. A normal reaction to this would be to go directly to the hospital. Instead, I pretended that it wasn't there. I never had thoughts of suicide, but I accepted death that day as if it had already happened. I was okay with not waking up, a feeling I had on a regular basis now. Death would be the easy road at this point. I had nothing and no one (I thought) who cared about me. I was at the lowest point I can remember. I lay face down in the cool grass, drifting in and out of consciousness, contemplating where my life had ended up until I fell asleep.

I don't know how long I was out, a couple of hours maybe. There was still daylight when I was woken by a sweet soothing voice. "Excuse me, sir." I opened my eyes for a few seconds and wondered who he was talking to because he obviously would not be talking to me. The voice crept closer, "Excuse me, sir, are you okay?" This time I was jarred awake and sat up abruptly. I waited for my eyes to focus on the two silhouettes standing between me and the bright sunlight. The man and woman slowly approached me as if I was some beat-down stray dog. They were an older couple, approximately in their sixties. They had that old-school hippie vibe that you would expect to see at a Grateful Dead show. Both wore hats and sunglasses and were wearing long sleeves in the middle of a scorching hot day. I was hesitant to say anything at first because I wasn't used to anyone wanting to talk to me, especially going out of their way to do so. The gentleman with his gray hair pulled back in a ponytail sat down next to me.

"How long have you been out here?" he asked with concern.

Thinking he was talking about how long I had been at the park, I replied, "Only a couple of hours."

He chuckled under his breath and re-worded his question. "How long have you been homeless?"

I grumbled, "A few months, I think."

It felt way longer than that, and I was unsure of the real answer. His words felt like a warm blanket on a cold night and instantly cut through my defense barriers.

"Don't you have any family that you can call that will help you out?"

I burst into tears as he was asking me, and it took me a couple of minutes to respond to him. "I do, but I am an addict that has completely destroyed everything."

This was the first real conversation that I had with anyone in a long time that wasn't based on getting and using drugs. He told me that he had observed me earlier sleeping on the grass and noticed my arm wrapped up in some old dirty gauze. He brought some new gauze and other medical supplies to help me clean up my arm. When we finished, he asked me if I believed in God. I had no answer to that question. At this point in my life, I had no business with an idea like that, and I figured if there was a God, why did he make me a homeless heroin addict? Why did he paralyze my arm in a motorcycle accident? Nonetheless, he asked if he and his wife could pray over me, and I didn't have the energy to put up a fight. I was completely content with feeling that love for those few minutes. I remember that interaction fondly because he never told me what I needed to do to straighten my life out. All he did was show some love and concern to a complete stranger when I needed it the most. After he and his wife crouched down to hug and pray with me, they gave me $30 and began to walk away. He turned back towards me mid-stride and said, "One day, you're going to have a lesson to teach someone; everything will work out the way it is meant to be." I didn't understand what he was saying until many years later. I was completely distracted by the money he gave me and was waiting for my moment to break free from the interaction. The beast needs to feed.

Without hesitancy, I ran back to the urban jungle to get some heroin. My next interaction was on the opposite side of the human kindness spectrum since you will trust anyone to get your next fix. I took part of the money and bought some cigarettes. As I stood outside the convenience store, I watched the people on the streets, picking out who the normal people were versus the drug addicts. This was an important skill to have to find what I needed. My last cell phone was long gone to call "the source," so I had to resort to approaching people on the street. I found my target and approached him confidently. He was a guy about my age wearing torn-up black jeans and an unbuttoned, tattered cream dress shirt. As I walked up to him, he immediately addressed my poorly wrapped hand.

"What's wrong with your hand?"

"It's infected," I calmly replied.

There's always an unspoken bond with fellow street dwellers, and we didn't need to qualify ourselves any further to each other. I told him I was in pain because of my hand and needed to find something to help me deal with it. He showed the same concern as the hippie couple did in the park and told me he could help.

I asked with caution, "Are you gonna burn me if I give you this 20?"

He assured me that he would never take advantage of someone in pain the way that I was. I should have known better since I would tell anyone whatever they wanted to hear to get what I wanted, but I was desperate and didn't have a choice.

"Wait right here," he said. "I'm gonna go straight to that motel across the street and will be right back."

I knew as soon as he walked across the street that I would never see him again. It didn't matter how many times I got burned by people. I continued to trust them if it meant getting what I needed because it was the only thing that mattered. I knew logically that people lie, cheat, and steal in this game, and I continued to do it, expecting different results because the power of heroin supersedes logic. I need to feel better NOW. I can't wait for a sure thing. I need this gorilla off my back immediately.

If finding someone to help me didn't work, then I resorted to conning someone else. There was a scam I used a few times to get some money. It went like this: I would walk into a store (generally a smoke shop) and frantically ask for help. When someone approached me, I would tell them I got robbed a few minutes before in the alley, and they took all my money. Using my wrapped hand as a tool, I would say that they had a knife and cut me with it, grabbing my phone and money. Pulling on people's heartstrings and arousing empathy would get them to hand over a couple of $20 dollar bills. My appearance supported the ruse. I looked like I had just been mugged. This was always a last-ditch effort to get some money, and it paid off for me a few times. Shame and guilt don't come into the equation.

I wish I could remember all the lies and negotiations I made with my mom. They all run together like a river of false promises draining into a sea of deceit. I convinced my mom to buy me a motel room for a week. I used my infected hand to persuade her. I spent one night there and had to go to the emergency room the next morning. I woke up with a pain I had never felt before. My entire right arm was three times the normal size, and it felt like my blood had been replaced with battery acid. Every time my heart beat, my whole body would throb in pain. I knew something was terribly wrong, and I immediately called my mom and told her what was going on. She was always calm in the scariest situations, but she was out of town, so my older brother Ryan was sent to pick me up and drive me to the emergency room. Who knows what was going through his mind when he saw me. He was very stoic and very concerned with my wellbeing, which was extremely comforting. Ryan never asked me questions or lectured me on what to do when I was in the throes of my battle. He would always support me, even if he didn't like what I was doing.

When I got to the emergency room, the reality of my life slapped me in the face. It was my second time at the hospital for a self-inflicted infection. The huge abscess on my hand was obvious, so the doctors ran a series of blood tests and determined I had staph and strep in my body. It was so swollen I couldn't determine where my hand ended and my fingers began. They told me the osteomyelitis (an infection in the bone) was back, a consequence of not taking care of it appropriately the last time. Every time I faced a situation like this, there was always one thought that came to mind: how long will it be before I start to get sick? The idea of dying from a blood infection was the last thing on my mind. I would only stay if they were going to give me some sort of opiate. Several nurses attempted to find a viable vein to put an IV in. After countless failed attempts, they had the anesthesiologist put a central PICC line in my neck. This would make administering drugs and collecting blood a whole lot easier. I just wanted all of this to be over with.

After they cleaned out all the infection in my right hand, I was ordered to complete four weeks of IV antibiotics to flush my system out. The hospital stay was agonizing, not because I was in physical pain but because I was riding a steady sick wave in body and mind. The weak Vicodin they were giving me wasn't going to cut it.

Addicts can be very resourceful, and that's exactly what I was. I watched the nurses day and night as they administered drugs to my central PICC line. I took note of what they were doing and exactly how they were doing it. All I needed was one of those plungers that hooked up to the device. One night I got lucky when a nurse left an empty one on the tray table. I quickly grabbed it and hid it in the bed with me. I started making calls from the hospital phone. I was desperately trying to locate anything I could put through the central line. Cocaine, meth, heroin, it didn't matter what it was at this point. I needed to scratch this deep itch if I was going to continue. I finally had a friend come to the hospital the next day, and he had a little bit of meth in his car. It never dawned on me how much of a problem it would be if I left the hospital to go out into the parking lot with all the devices still attached to me. I quickly grabbed what I needed and headed back into my room. All the nurses and security guards were walking the halls looking for me. Apparently, it's dangerous to get up and walk out with a central PICC line in your neck. They were not happy, to say the least. In my usual defensive fashion, I lied. I told them I needed some fresh air and that it was no big deal. Taking responsibility for anything was not my strong suit.

After my disappearing act, the terms of my stay quickly changed. The first few days I was in the hospital, I noticed people sitting watch 24 hours a day. I was curious why these "babysitters" were randomly placed in front of different rooms. I found out that these people were hired to keep track of patients. It became clear when they assigned one of these people to watch me. The irritation in me was at boiling point as I realized that my sneaky behavior wouldn't be able to continue. The amount of time and energy that I put into acting sober, and putting on a trustworthy appearance, was baffling. Anytime I got pushed into a corner where I wasn't in control, the flight or fight instinct would be activated. As I lay in that hospital bed, I knew that I wouldn't be sticking around. My mom and grandmother came to check on me after I got busted. As soon as I heard their voices coming down the hall, I pretended to be asleep, so I didn't have to explain myself and, more importantly, so I could plot my escape. As soon as they left, I looked at my babysitter and told him that I would be leaving. I would have left without saying anything, but I needed to get this line out of my neck. The nurses pleaded with me not to go, but my mind was made up way before that conversation.

I briskly walked into the busy city and knew exactly where to go. It's hard to explain the singular mind of an addict. The need to get high was louder than the noise around me. Louder than any thought or physical sensation could be. My feet were on autopilot toward the last known destination of relief. I didn't know if my friend would still be in the same spot, but it didn't matter. I was going to try regardless. I had complete faith that what I needed would be sitting in a motel room off Virginia Street. Completely unaware of the danger to my health, I confidently walked up to the door and knocked. THANK GOD he was there. Relief at last.

Back to the grind, the following weeks were business as usual. Locked up in a motel room with my fair-weather junkies, pretending that nothing else existed. Day in and day out, sunup to sundown, chasing the allusive serenity that heroin brought me. To keep this state of mind, you must adapt to the surroundings and find new hustles constantly. I've sold a lot of drugs in my life, but heroin was by far the most dangerous and unpredictable. Getting ripped off or robbed was a common occurrence. One day, when I was doing my usual rounds, I came across an unhappy customer. I was always on my feet, so it was easy for others to run up to me at any given time. This guy, nicknamed "trouble" (for obvious reasons), accused me of ripping him off on his last sack. I told him I had no idea what he was talking about. Now, I ripped him off, but that's the name of the game when you are trying to stay well and sell dope. He asked me what I was going to do to make it right, and I told him to go fuck himself.

Rule number one when selling drugs on the street is don't ever turn your back on anyone and leave yourself open for attack. When you sell a drug like heroin, it gives you this false sense of power, like you are untouchable and nothing bad will ever happen. That statement feels like an oxymoron now.

Trouble proceeded to pull out an extendable police baton and hit me so hard on the jaw from behind that I never felt a thing. He knocked me out cold on the sidewalk in broad daylight. The only reason I know what weapon he used is because I heard about it from other people. I went into a very confusing dream state where I could see the surrounding area but couldn't hear anything going on. I was floating about six feet above the sidewalk and watched the ambulance pull up. I remember thinking to myself, "Hmm, I wonder who got hurt." All of a sudden, I opened my eyes to a police officer standing above me with the sun directly behind his head. As I came to, I had no idea what had happened and noticed a large amount of blood on the sidewalk that I was lying on. I got knocked out so hard that my head dove straight into the concrete and split the top of my forehead straight back into my hairline. They had to put eighteen stitches in my head at the hospital. I was fortunate because I had an eight-ball of dope in my pocket when it happened. Luckily, when you are a victim of a crime, they don't tend to search you or ask any questions.

Any normal person would stop after an incident like this, but I wasn't a normal person. The disease of addiction allows you to forget the pain and suffering of each terrifying low point. The doctor stitched me up, and I was on my way back to the streets in a few short hours. They even gave me a script of Vicodin, so I felt like I had won. The doctor advised me to come back in eight days to get the stitches taken out. I had no intention of following through. I walked around with those stitches for well over a month. I was walking around downtown Reno when my mom spotted me from her car and pulled over. The look on her face when she saw me was like I had died right in front of her. She turned ghostly white when I explained to her what had happened. She offered to get me a stitch removal kit and bought me some Starbucks. I wanted to ask her for help so badly at that moment, but I just wasn't done. My brain was screaming inside a soundproof room. I couldn't admit defeat. I believed that I could get myself out of this terrible cycle. The shame consumed me like quicksand and made me want to end our conversation as quickly as possible. Out of sight, out of mind. That's the addict's way of solving all problems.

The following month was what I imagined hell would be like. I had nowhere to go and found myself sleeping under a bridge with multiple other lost souls. We were a band of nomads that nobody paid attention to; we were invisible. A lot of people used nicknames on the street. I don't know if this was to hide who they really were or to dehumanize the already gut-wrenching experience of trying to survive minute to minute. I tried to build some resemblance of a home with milk crates I stole from the back of the Walgreens above the overpass. The noise from the freeway was deafening to the point where it would block out your thoughts and provide a barrier from the outside world. Unfortunately, that was a perfect environment for others to steal your shit when you fell asleep.

The first night I slept under the bridge, I made the fatal mistake of taking my backpack off and sleeping next to it. It was gone by morning, and I quickly learned that I was living in a dog-eat-dog world. No one could be trusted, and nobody was your friend. You only kept what you had attached to you or had in your pockets. I became a master of hiding things throughout the city that I needed to keep. Things like phone chargers, battery packs, clothes, shoes, underwear, sleeping bag, jackets, and canned food were all things that would be snatched up if they weren't stored somewhere safe. I craved human interaction, but no one was there to lean on or to be helpful. We were all trying to barely survive while constantly staying high, not exactly a recipe for strong community living. People only wanted to be around you if you could offer them something or help them get something. Every man fends for themselves. It felt like being locked in a prison the size of a city and constantly looking for the key to get out. It was the meaning of hopelessness.

Humans have a stunning ability to adjust to any situation they are faced with. Resilience and resourcefulness were my driving forces to stay alive. Things got progressively harder when the weather started to change. It was November, and it was becoming unbearable to be outside. I would go from casino to casino to stay warm. I would sleep in the bathroom stalls and do my drugs there. Security caught on quickly, and I was slowly blacklisted from all the casinos downtown.

I remember the last night I slept on the street very well. It was about 30 degrees outside, and I was trying to sleep with a sleeping bag over my body. As I lay there, I could feel the mice trying to get in the sleeping bag as they crawled all over my body. I would violently shake them off, only for them to return minutes later. They were cold and hungry like me. I still have nightmares about it.

The next day I called my mom from a random number and made a deal with her. I begged her to get me a motel room for a few days, and then I'd go to treatment. She said she would call around to see if she could find a rehab bed. I don't know if I wanted to be sober, but I didn't want to be homeless in winter. This was another desperate manipulation to get out of my current circumstance. Mom fell for it again. By the time she picked me up and took me to her house, I was already becoming sick. I couldn't resist the usual pillaging of her personal belongings. I found four Percocet in her bathroom and got a little relief to get me through Thanksgiving. The next day I was headed to an inpatient 30-day rehab program for the first time. It was 2016.

Chapter Seven

Elko: Lisa

"The most important thing in life is to dare.
The most complicated thing in life is to be afraid."
Shimon Peres

"I want to make a change. I want to get clean." Gerad called me that November from another number I didn't recognize. He had told me this before after close calls, lost cars, lost lives, and the fear of losing his own. The weather was beginning to get cold. I was no longer paying for a place for him to stay, and the loss of his girlfriend, who had been arrested and placed into a program a few months earlier, left him with no other option. I occasionally received a text from him, and I had finally come to the realization that I had to say no and remain firm if I was going to save him. I created a text I copied and pasted over and over when I would receive a request from him: "I am not going to support you when you are using. If you want to get clean, I will pick you up anytime, anywhere." I would get responses like, "You're not even going to buy me food?", "Thanks for nothing," or "You don't care anymore." I would keep copying and pasting the same message to each response. Sometimes I was shaking, sometimes crying; it was the hardest thing I had done, but I was emphatic, and he knew he was out of options.

His only request this time was for him to spend Thanksgiving with us before he went. After years of manipulation, I sighed and wondered if this was just another way to get off the streets for a few nights. He had tried and failed several outpatient programs, refusing to go someplace where he didn't know anyone or where he would be locked up. There were always excuses not to try.

It had been a while since I had called any programs. It was such a frustrating process with so few beds available in our state. I had left hundreds of messages over the previous four years and only got a few calls returned, always with the same bad news. My expectations were low, but I had to try. I grabbed my list and left messages for New Frontiers, Bristlecone, Vitality, and on and on, seven facilities in all. I had learned the right things to say to make the admission "high risk." He checked all the boxes to be considered urgent. The only thing that would have increased his chances was being pregnant or coming from jail. Yes, being in prison and addicted makes you a higher priority than being homeless and addicted. Go figure. I received a call within an hour. I was shocked and giddy at the same time. No one had ever called me back so quickly, let alone ask the question, "Tell me what's going on with your son?"

It was an admissions counselor for a rehab with two locations in the state. She said she had one bed open, but it was in the Elko facility, a four-and-a-half-hour drive from Reno.

"Could you get him here the day after Thanksgiving?"

I was stunned and didn't say anything for a moment.

"Ma'am?"

"Yes, yes, yes, I will get him there."

She said she would email me some forms to fill out, directions, and a list of what to bring.

"Oh, and one last thing, he needs to detox before he gets here."

If a rehab had a bed, I figured there must have been a seismic shift in the addiction industry in Nevada. Getting into detox would be a piece of cake.

There was never a good way to contact Gerad. Phones were like currency for addicts, and he rarely had the same number for long. It was a nail-biting 24 hours, but I also knew he had no resources, so he would have to call me sooner or later. I told him I would pick him up, and he gave me a time and place. Gerad had been homeless for a while and looked and smelled like it. It was still a punch in the gut to see him this way. I took him home to get showered and fed while I called to see if he could get into detox. I first tried a new facility in town because I thought it might be easier to get in. I had been excited for the community to finally have an alternative. Although they advertised addiction detox and treatment, the lady on the phone told me they weren't set up yet to accept patients with substance abuse. The frustrations of getting help marched on. I reverted to calling West Hills, the facility he had used twice before. Making an appointment was surprisingly easy. Maybe things were looking up. I knew we only had a few hours before he would be in withdrawals, so as soon as he was cleaned up, we headed out to what I hoped would be the beginning of the end of this nightmare.

Nothing had changed at the detox facility since our first time. It felt like a time capsule of our ordeal. This would be Gerad's third admission. The wait was surprisingly short, with no one in the waiting room or the intake rooms in the back. It seemed too easy, and I seriously considered that my memories of previous experiences were exaggerated in my mind. Since we had the place to ourselves, we sat out in the middle instead of going into one of the interview rooms. Gerad had always been treated compassionately and respectfully by the counselors conducting the admission interview. I had no reason to expect otherwise until she asked her first questions.

"Why are you here today?"

I explained that he finally had a bed waiting for him in rehab, and they required him to detox before admission.

"Are you in withdrawal? When did you last use? You don't look very sick. What are your symptoms?"

She asked them rapid-fire without making eye contact. The relief I had felt for the last 24 hours began to dissipate. Her tone was condescending as she looked down at his paperwork. Gerad explained that he was nauseous, achy, and anxious. As she looked at her nails, yes, seriously, she explained that Medicaid wouldn't pay for detox unless he was in full-blown withdrawals and sick enough for admission. I stared at her in silence. Finally, I said, "Are you kidding me? For the first time in four years, I have a bed waiting for him, and the only requirement is that he detox before he gets there. You seem bored. Is there someone else we can talk to?" She looked up at me and said she would talk to her supervisor, "But I don't think he will get approved."

I kept silently repeating to myself, "My God, My God, My God." I couldn't believe we could be this close, and some idiot, uncaring, patronizing twenty-something would be our obstacle. She had to be new, or the facility was under new management. Maybe she was an intern? Maybe the new facility had hired all the good people, and she was the best they could get.

I looked at Gerad and said, "Holy hell, you have got to be kidding me." This experience was the opposite of our previous ones. I felt like I was in the twilight zone. She was only gone for a few minutes when she returned and, without sitting down, let us know that Gerad wasn't sick enough for admission.

"Like I said, you can bring him back if he gets worse."

I felt numb.

"Why would we be here if he wasn't in withdrawal? Do you actually believe people come here wanting to scam the system for a few glorious days locked up in this place? If you turn us away, we will lose his only decent chance to get clean."

She was unmoved and just looked past us. I grabbed my bag, told Gerad to come on, and stomped out of there.

I was seething. I wanted to scream, cry, or punch something; I wanted to punch that arrogant bitch. I knew I had to remain calm on the outside for Gerad. I didn't want him to bolt. He looked at me and said, "It's okay, Mom, the withdrawals aren't as bad this time. I was using less because I had no way to buy it." I looked at him, and we both knew it wouldn't be that easy. I immediately started thinking of ways to keep him occupied for three days, or what I could give him, or where we could go. I felt desperate. I knew Valium or

Xanax would work because they had given it to him during detox. I texted a friend I knew had a prescription for Xanax for anxiety. "Any chance you could spare a few Xanax?" She quickly replied she hadn't been using it and no longer had the prescription. I asked Gerad if he knew where we could get some. Funny question. We drove to an apartment complex, and I gave him some money with strict instructions. "Promise me you'll only get what we agreed to, and be quick." He nodded and ran across the street. He came back quickly and showed me the pills. Just enough to get him through. I gave him one and kept the rest.

He said the girl was his friend, and he told her he was going to rehab. She gave him a big hug and told him she knew he would make it. A young guy he knew was sitting on the couch and asked Gerad if he wanted to buy some tools. "I'm going to get clean too. Just need to sell these tools and get some money together." Gerad told him no and wished him luck. He told me addicts always talk about getting clean. All the time, to each other, their families, and strangers on the street. That young man was dead before Gerad entered rehab. It was not the first person he knew who had overdosed, and it wouldn't be the last.

We had a pleasant Thanksgiving, and Gerad seemed upbeat. I watched him like a hawk, checking on him when he was sleeping to make sure he didn't slip away. I hid all the cell phones, landlines, car keys, money, prescriptions, and anything of value. It had become a routine whenever he was in the house. We left early the next morning, and I told Gerad to grab a pillow and try to sleep. We drove the four-and-a-half hours to Elko, hopeful and in slight disbelief. We had tried for so long that it almost seemed anti-climactic. Gerad packed what little he owned in a backpack, and I added the other required items from the list I was emailed to a duffle bag.

When we pulled up, Gerad got out of the car, grabbed a small bag out of the backpack, and told me to get rid of it. He said it was his kit. He had held onto it until the very last minute, and I could tell it was hard for him to turn it over. He turned away and lit his last cigarette. I opened the kit. There were several syringes, alcohol swabs, and needles. I walked over to a nearby trash can and threw it away. As I walked back toward Gerad, I wondered how many other people had used that same trash can to try and start fresh.

As we walked toward the one-story yellow building, I was not impressed. It seemed neglected, sitting alone in a dirt parking lot. I could see fencing around the right side but nothing else that would keep people from leaving. The lobby was very small, with just two chairs and a counter. Pamphlets covered the counter and some of the walls. The carpet was the kind you used to see on back porches and looked to have been a rust color at one time. Now it just looked brown. A door stood shut on our left, and what appeared to be an entrance to a small office was straight ahead. Gerad dropped his bags and sat down. I could tell he was anxious. He leaned his head against the wall and turned to the right, eyes open and apprehensive. A heavy-set lady with bright red hair and horn-rimmed glasses on a chain greeted us. I was hoping the admissions counselor would be there, so I asked about her. I was told she worked out of her home in another state. That, and the looks of the place, gave me an uneasy feeling, but I couldn't turn back now. I signed the paperwork and gave them a check to start his personal account for various snacks, toiletries, and a vape. Most treatment centers have a strict no-smoking policy, but this one allowed vaping.

A blonde lady came in from the office and asked Gerad several questions. She asked about banned items he may have in his belongings, if he was in withdrawal, and explained the rules. He answered all her questions, and she seemed satisfied. She told me there would be a ten-day black-out period, and Gerad would not be allowed to contact anyone. She turned to me and asked me to say goodbye. Gerad stood up, and I gave him a hug. "I love you. You can do this." He gave me a perfunctory nod and shuffled off behind the closed door. The lady behind the counter said, "Don't worry, mama, he'll be OK." I walked out and got into the car with my husband. I immediately told him I didn't feel good about leaving Gerad there.

114

I put on my seat belt, took one last look at the door, and sighed. We drove back to Reno, mostly silent, me in deep thought. I prayed that this would work.

Gerad was placed alone in a room in the detox section of the facility. He was allowed to write letters at first but not call. I received two and then finally a phone call. He told me his detox hadn't been too bad, and he now had a room with another guy younger than him. He was excited to have a comfortable mattress. That made me smile. He said the place wasn't too bad, and he liked the Director. There were several people in there from Reno, and two had taken off, running out the door one night after dinner. We both laughed, wondering if they understood the geography between Elko and Reno. It was cold, desolate, and dark. Obviously, they didn't have a plan. He said local women came in and cooked for them, and the food was really good. He seemed content for now and even said he didn't mind group sessions too much. He said he would be allowed visitors on Christmas Day, and he was excited for us to come. That was three weeks away. He called once a week and continued to seem upbeat. Hope crept in, but I felt I'd know more when I saw him.

His oldest brother, my husband, and I made the trek on Christmas Day. We were allowed to bring presents, but most would have to go home with us. Only two of us were allowed in, so we decided it should be Ryan and me. My husband spent the next several hours at a local casino watching football. I still choke up thinking of him driving all that way to sit there on Christmas Day alone.

Gerad was genuinely happy to see us. We were able to eat lunch with him and all the clients and their families. Many had no one to visit. I couldn't imagine what that must be like for them. Everyone was excited and loud when we were lining up to go into the cafeteria. One of the counselors tried to get their attention to tell them the rules. I don't think anyone heard him. Gerad spoke up loudly, asking for everyone's attention. I got emotional, swelling with pride. He was a leader. He'd come a long way from sleeping under a bridge a few months before. After lunch, he showed us his room, and we met his roommate, who was excitedly eating the Christmas candy the staff had placed in Christmas stockings. He reminded me of a child on Christmas morning.

We moved to a small lounge area with a couch and chairs. Gerad was animated and talkative. I sat and stared in wonder. He seemed like his old self but better. He opened his gifts and was genuinely thankful for them all. He told us that the Director had asked him to teach some art classes to the clients. I asked him about the next steps. He said that at the beginning of January, he would move to a house in town with other clients from the program. He would stay there for six months and continue aftercare at the facility. He had been told everyone at the house had to get a job, drug test daily, and attend meetings. He was anxious to move to the next step. The visit was short but thrilling. I told him I would be back after he moved into the Sober Living House. We hugged and smiled. It was a good day.

After his move to the house, his daughter and I were able to visit several times. Gerad did his best to reconnect with her. I brought him his guitar and an iPad. He had been trying to get a job, but it had proven difficult. He had a misdemeanor arrest for petty theft that showed up on any background checks. He even pleaded his case in front of the City Council, hoping to become a cab driver. He spent most of his time at the local library, which was close to the sober house since he didn't have a car. He finally found a job at a grocery store.

After six months at the house, he was once again anxious to move to the next step and gain some independence. We bought him an old Toyota pick-up so he could finally get around, get to work, and attend meetings. He soon began looking for places of his own. We both agreed it was best for him to stay in Elko and away from the temptations in Reno. He found a cute little yellow house and was excited to move in. I loaded a U-Haul with the things of his I still had, along with some extra furniture. He had been so excited to move that he had bought a blow-up mattress and began living there before his stuff arrived. We set him up, and he was happy to be surrounded by memories from his life before everything went off the rails. He liked his job, was working on eating healthy, and had started walking for exercise. He was losing the weight he had gained since getting sober. I don't know when things derailed, but it happened long before I realized it.

He called once, saying he had been gambling. He reached out to a counselor at the rehab for help. He was working so many shifts at work that he was no longer attending the four-hour-long meetings required in aftercare. Once again, he was having trouble telling people no. He began smoking pot to relieve his anxiety. I had sent him a bracelet with his one-year sobriety date on it. I found out later he hadn't made it a year.

When he came home at Christmas, I thought he looked fantastic. He was engaged and helpful, excited about his job and his life. He had already begun to use meth by then to stay awake for the extra and double shifts he continued to take on. I honestly had no idea. He texted me in March and said he couldn't do it anymore. He was going to sell his phone to get the money for heroin. I begged him to let me come get him or buy him a train ticket. I knew once the phone was gone, I would lose contact. By the end of March, he was arrested for possession and put in jail. He begged me to bail him out so he could save his job. I did, and not only did he not save his job, but he was arrested again on April 19th. Two arrests, two felonies. He wasn't getting out anytime soon.

My next trip to Elko was to pick up what pieces were left of Gerad's broken life. His car had been impounded, and his belongings scattered amongst acquaintances, so I brought his brother to help load what was left in the truck and drive it back to Reno. I wasn't allowed to visit Gerad in jail yet, but I learned about his rapid decline as I made the rounds to gather what I could, including his truck. He had made a lot of friends, especially at work, and they were shocked and angry to find out he was an addict. They had noticed the weight loss and sudden requests to borrow money and believed all his excuses until they read about his arrest.

I headed to the impound lot after gathering what identification paperwork we could find in his things. We pulled in and spotted his forest green 4Runner right away. The place was on the outskirts of town and looked like a junkyard straight out of a movie, with a skinny three-legged dog and a dilapidated building. A crooked sign said, "Office." Only the O and the P were lit up on the open sign. As I entered, the lady behind the desk looked up and cheerfully asked how she could help.

"I've come to pick up my son's truck. The police said you had it."

"What kind of truck, hon?

I grabbed the registration I had found and handed it over. She checked it over and then looked at me and sighed.

"I'm so happy you came. I've been trying to find the owner's family. The police didn't have an emergency contact. Is Gerad your son?"

"Yes. How do you know Gerad?"

"This is the second time his truck was impounded. He came and got it two weeks ago. I was really worried about him. He looked really thin and sick; he could barely stand. I asked him if he was alright and if he should call someone to come get him. He said he was fine and there wasn't anyone to call anyway. I was worried when the truck came in again. He mentioned he worked at Smith's, so I called the manager, but they said he didn't work there anymore."

I stared at her, speechless. Her empathy startled me out of my numbness. I had been going through the motions, just trying to make it through yet another setback in Gerad's decline. Yet, at the moment when I felt all hope was lost, this complete stranger had been searching for me because she was worried about another complete stranger. Tears welled up in my eyes, but no words came out.

"Is everything OK? Is your son OK?"

I couldn't remember the last time I had let myself feel enough to cry. I remember thinking that it was people like her that made me believe living in a small town would be good for Gerad. Afraid the floodgates would open, all I could choke out was, "Thank you for asking. He'll be OK."

I knew that wasn't true, but it felt necessary to put her mind at ease. I paid the bill and told her thanks again. So often on this journey with Gerad, I felt like I had to convince people to care, but people can surprise you in the most unexpected places, like a junkyard in Elko, Nevada.

Gerad spent five months in the Elko County Jail. His hand infection returned as soon as he started using, and they only had a nurse and a PA to see him. They offered antibiotics and Advil. I was able to schedule a visit coinciding with his first hearing. His attorney talked to the DA, and they agreed to work on getting him into treatment. They brought him into the hallway where I was waiting. He was in handcuffs and dressed in an orange jumpsuit that looked two sizes too big. He looked so small but managed a slight wave and a smile. It was heartbreaking. I wondered how many times one person's heart could break before the pieces were no longer able to mend.

Chapter Seven

Elko: Gerad

"There were two lovely choices.
One of them meant giving up every chance
of a decent life forever…And the other one
scared me out of my mind."
Fredrick Pohl

It was the middle of November 2016 when it was getting bitter cold outside. I contacted my mom because I was tired of being tired again. I had nowhere to go. After being homeless on the streets for six months, I was convinced I would never go back to shooting heroin and meth. I would learn later that no number of dark experiences will ever be enough for a disease that requires a spiritual overhaul to overcome.

The Nevada Department of Transportation finally kicked us out from under the bridge. The day we got kicked out, there was a group of us huddled in a circle, and they were telling us that we needed to grab our shit and exit the bridge immediately. I remember trying to shoot up in my leg as the guy stared right at me. I became extremely brazen in these last moments. The shame of hiding anything evaporates when you reach the depths of hell.

I negotiated with my mom to buy me a motel room for a couple of nights, with the promise of going to treatment. I would have kept using if I had the means to, but I grew tired of trying to swindle and steal my next high. My mom picked me up, and I was on an emotional rollercoaster. I wanted to be sober without having to endure the withdrawal. No matter how many times I went through the agony of getting off opiates, I always found myself right back in the middle of it. I had been in a constant state of sickness for the past month, so I told myself that it wouldn't be that bad this time. The peace of getting high ended a long time ago.

By the time I took a shower and changed clothes, my mind immediately changed. I wanted one more rush. Anything to take the sickness away. I searched through my mom's bathroom; she started putting her Percocet in different bottles the last time I was scrounging around. I knew I had to check every bottle she had. I was desperately looking and hoping there would be anything. Finally, I found about five Percocet and took all of them at once. The relief took hold instantly, and I sat on the couch, waiting for my mom to get back from whatever she was doing.

When Mom came in the door, she told me with excitement, "Great news, you have a bed in Elko. We just need to get you to detox." I was thinking, "Oh shit, there's no way detox is going to take me now; I just took a whole bunch of pills." I couldn't tell her the truth, though. I went ahead with the plan and drove down to the detox with her. This would be my third visit to this institution. It felt like a loop in a bad dream. The process was expedited this time, and I was hoping against all hope that they would accept me. The only thing I remember from this visit was how callused the intake lady was. She had no interest in looking at me and kept her nose buried in the paperwork. She asked me questions like a robot, and I could tell it wouldn't be a favorable outcome. She told us to come back when I was withdrawing, and my mom turned red. She always did a great job at hiding her emotions, but I could see the anger and frustration this time.

When we got back in the car, I kept telling her, "The withdraws aren't as bad this time. I'll be fine." She didn't know I was still high. I wanted her to believe in me so badly. I wanted that more than I wanted to be sober. I told her I could get Xanax, and we could just go through the process at her house. Surprisingly, she agreed and took me to a house to get it. We were two sides of the same desperate coin. She watched me carefully over the next couple of days and gave me Xanax when needed. I never got used to feeling like a criminal in my own mother's house. They would hide everything from me when I was around. I was the creator of this misery, but I still felt disgusted by it. The only reason I knew they hid everything from me was because I would lurk around the house looking for an escape plan. I always needed a contingency in case things didn't work out.

We left early in the morning and headed toward salvation. I felt awful and tried to sleep the whole way there. I took a pillow and blanket and hid in the backseat. The body aches and restless legs gave me mixed signals, and I forced myself to sleep but at the same time be wide awake. I called it doing sleep karate. I constantly wanted to move my limbs and body back and forth. There was no such thing as a comfortable position. My mom was mostly silent the whole ride. I was terrified when we arrived, this was my first time in treatment, and I had no idea what to expect. I handed my mom my kit, which was a sunglass case full of syringes and alcohol wipes. It was the only thing that I held onto while being homeless on the street. It was this weird cathartic severance. My life had been reduced to this one makeshift sentimental package, and it was hard to hand it over.

The treatment center was bland and nothing to write home about. It was far from the luxury treatment centers I had heard about. They had a ten-foot barbed wire fence around the property that made it feel like a prison. I was put into the detox wing of the treatment center with a nurse 24 hours a day. I gutted out my withdrawal and watched a bunch of movies until I was ready to be moved into the general population. The idea of being sober was scary, and I didn't know what to expect or do. This would be my first time ever hearing the 12 steps of recovery.

A counselor named Tamara was assigned to manage my case. She was the first person that showed genuine interest in me outside of my family. The most memorable thing was the memory foam mattresses. God, I hadn't slept that good in years. I was housed with about 25 other men and women from all walks of life. I had hope for the first time in a long time and was excited about the future. This was a padded environment where I would be safe, or so I thought. I had this delusion that everyone that made it to treatment would leave and be sober for the rest of their lives. I knew if I made it this far, I would have a chance. My delusion was smashed when the counselors said that only about 2% would make it. That was a hard number for me to swallow as I looked around the room at the friendly faces I was becoming close to. Author Chuck Palahniuk references the idea of "single-serving friends" in his book *Fight Club*. The idea is that you were only friends if the circumstance which you're in lasted. This couldn't be truer for detoxes, rehabs, and jails. I became fast friends with many people, never to see them again after our experience was over. I also experienced how fragile and fatal this disease was and is. My roommate was a guy in his early 20s. I became close to him, and we talked about our dreams and hopes for the future. After treatment was over, he overdosed and died in a dilapidated motel in Elko. I was aware that people were dying from addiction, but it became more magnified in a treatment setting. This was a 30-day program, and I thought that was excruciatingly long. I later found that I needed something way longer than 30 days.

My next phase was to live in a sober house run by the same people. This was a six-month commitment, and I was excited about life for the first time. Even though I was away from home, I knew in my heart that I had a good chance. I gained enough knowledge to move forward, but knowledge alone wasn't enough to keep me sober. I got a job at a grocery store and saved up enough money to move out on my own. I wanted to be self-sustaining. I wanted that more than I wanted to be sober, which proved to be a mistake. The padded environment of treatment and sober living kept me on track for a while, but as soon as I moved into my own place, things started to take a turn.

I started working graveyard shifts on top of random other day shifts. I thought, "Man, this would be a lot easier to work overnight if I had something to help me out." I convinced myself that I was experiencing anxiety and explained that to my mom. Nevada had just legalized marijuana for recreational use, and that made my argument of why I needed it much more logical. I always had a reservation that I could just smoke weed, and everything would be okay. I learned slowly over time that addiction is a progressive disease. Once an addict makes it to shooting heroin and meth, that is always where an addict ends up, no matter what they put in their body. I had a good life once upon a time with weed, and I wanted that back more than anything. I held onto that for years. It was easy to find from fellow coworkers. I could find drugs anywhere in the world if I wanted to. As soon as I was on the prowl, it didn't take long to find some meth. I had the delusion that I could control it if I stuck to the meth. I told myself that I would only use it to work and I would only smoke weed when I was off. I had intricate plans and intentions that I could never stick to.

I held this lifestyle for about six months before things started to go off the rails. I met more people in the drug game in Elko, and before I knew it, I was right back in the middle of where I never wanted to be again. I became a daily user and would find myself nodding off at work because I had been up for days. One time I fell asleep standing up while operating a pallet jack. My reality was beginning to break apart. People at work noticed my extreme weight loss and began asking questions about it. I told them that I was exercising a lot and eating healthier. They would say, "You look sick. You don't look healthy at all." This was the pattern that I experienced many times. Telling everyone that it was all okay while rotting from the inside out.

I started gambling, which goes hand in hand with meth use. I could not afford to pay the rent at my house and was evicted. I was back to shooting meth and heroin when I told myself I would never do that again. This was the insanity of addiction playing out once more. I moved all my stuff into a hotel casino in Elko, and what happened next would finally push me to make drastic changes in my life.

It was a Saturday. I had to work all day dope sick and was itching to get off and make my way to the hotel where all my drugs were. I let a girl that I was hanging out with borrow my 4-Runner while I was at work, and she was late to pick me up. If there is one thing you can count on, it's how unreliable drugs make people act when they are actively using them. She finally picked me up, and I remember being so sweaty and achy that I only wanted one thing, a shot of heroin. When we pulled up to the hotel, my friend wanted to wait in the car while I ran upstairs. I didn't think anything of it. I just wanted some relief. I walked into the hotel and made a couple of turns to a long hallway where my room was located. I could see a maid and a security guard standing outside my room. I got closer to the prize when the security guard ducked inside my room. Now, any normal person in this situation would think that was odd and probably keep walking by as though nothing happened, but I was determined. I burst into my room and was met by a man, well over 6 feet tall, with a dark complexion, and wearing a blue security uniform. He was standing by my pile of drugs on the table. I acted like I was lost and said, "This isn't my room!" That was a ridiculous claim since I opened the door with a key card. He calmly explained to me that it was illegal to do drugs in the hotel. I thought, yeah, no shit. He said that Elko police had been called, and they were on the way. He left the room abruptly, and I was alone.

I gathered the drugs and quickly whipped up a shot and tried to find a vein. This was impossible because of dehydration and over-flowing adrenaline. After a few minutes, I heard a loud pounding on the door. "Elko Police Department." I had a sneaking suspicion that they weren't going away, so I decided to muscle the shot in my arm. I viewed muscling as a waste of dope, but these were desperate times. I waited about 30 seconds before I answered the door. I knew I was going to jail.

My mom was always the first person I called when I got to jail. Her number was burned into my mind from years of desperate calls from random phones. Over the years, she sounded less and less surprised, but I was grateful that she always answered. I started the manipulation by telling her everything she wanted to hear to get bailed out. I cannot remember all the lies, but I know I told her I wanted to save my job and that I would stay at my coworker's house. She got me out, and none of those things worked. The plan went sideways, as usual.

It turns out that Elko prints the daily arrests in the local paper, and everyone knew what I got charged with. Three felony counts don't win over the hearts of the public. Possession of heroin, meth, and needles. Seeing that in the paper made me feel subhuman. I went and scored the night I got out of jail. I walked all the way across the city, back to where my 4-Runner was and drove it to the dope house. I never had any intentions of doing what I told my mom I would.

After you get arrested in a small town, all the cops know who you are and what vehicle you drive. Over the next few weeks, I got pulled over at least ten times. I was playing this cat-and-mouse game and thought I knew my rights well enough to keep getting out of these bullshit traffic stops. They would always ask to search my car, and I would refuse. They even seized my car to search it and made me walk from the scene. They were out for blood, and eventually, they beat me at the chess game.

There was a moment of clarity the second time I got arrested on April 19th, 2018. I spent hours in a casino parking lot getting high and listening to music. I made no effort to hide my drugs before I started driving down the road. I passed a cruiser that had someone pulled over already. I looked in my rear-view mirror and saw the cop quickly jump back in his car and flip around, heading towards me. I thought, "Well, this is it." He pulled me over, and before I knew it, there was a second cop behind me. It was the K-9 unit. They pulled me over with a drug dog in tow. They were going in for the kill, and I was tired of fighting. They pulled me out of the car, searched it, and sent the drug dog a signal. I murmured, "Just take me to jail. Let's get this show on the road." It was freezing outside, and I think they enjoyed letting me shake out there while they dug through the nooks and crannies of my car. I was a huge thorn in their side for the past month, and I could see the satisfaction in their eyes as I stood there with my hands cuffed behind my back. They were like Dobermans licking their chops at some raw meat. The cop that was watching me kept telling me how he liked to run marathons for fun. The provoking didn't work. I was utterly done at this point. My body was an empty shell. When they put me in the back of the cruiser, I felt a sense of relief. I knew deep down that this was the turning point for me. I sure as hell knew they weren't letting me out this time. I spent the next five months in Elko County Jail.

Chapter Eight

Incarceration: Lisa

"In the middle of difficulty lies opportunity."
Albert Einstein

Being in jail has a way of making what you want in life clearer, or in Gerad's case, what you don't want. The first time he ended up in jail, I immediately thought, "I have to get him out. He can't survive in there." By the third or fourth time, it was a blessing and the best I could hope for at that point. After his arrests in Elko in 2018, he had to detox in jail. The treatment is always the same: a cell by yourself, a sandwich, and Tylenol. With so many drug-related arrests in this country, I assumed jails would have seen the need for medical assistance, but it's not exactly a crisis in the public eye unless it's your son, your daughter, or your spouse. Addiction is the only disease treated as a criminal act. I'm not referring to what they do because of the addiction, like theft, robbery, and vagrancy; I'm talking about drug possession or paraphernalia. Four of Gerad's felonies listed on his paperwork in Elko were for possession of drug paraphernalia. There isn't much sympathy from law enforcement or anyone else.

One ironic advantage of jail was that Gerad could call regularly, and I could see him when I drove over for court appearances. I hadn't had that kind of consistency in years. I encouraged him to ask for medical treatment and, at the very least, get on an antibiotic for his hand. Resources are limited in jail, and I implored him to be persistent. The biggest disadvantage of being in a small county jail was they had even more limited resources and very little interest in helping an addict. Generally, they hire a nurse, a physician's assistant, a long-retired doctor, or a dentist to take care of the inmate's needs. I admire those that do it, but it's not considered admirable. The pay is poor and the schedule inconsistent, so the positions generally go unfilled. Gerad had developed a lot of dental issues, mainly from being cold cocked by an angry customer on the street, and several of his teeth were broken. He told me the last guy the jail sent to the dentist had the wrong tooth pulled. Needless to say, Gerad said he'd tough it out.

Elko would be the first time Gerad spent any real time incarcerated. He had been arrested previously for petty theft and a couple of other misdemeanors. I can no longer remember for what, but he only spent a couple of nights in jail. I still remember getting that first call. He asked me to bail him out and said he'd never make it if he had to stay in jail. He was in a full-blown panic. I felt terrible for him and put up the five hundred dollars, and he was out within a few hours, disappearing once again. Not sure what else I expected. The next time he went to jail was when the police had called looking for him, and I told them where he was hanging out in hopes they would find him and save his life. I honestly didn't think they would find him. He called immediately with the same song and dance, but this time I said no. He kept calling me back. I knew part of the panic was real. The idea of having no access to drugs and getting dope sick scared the hell out of him. I'm sure being locked up had something to do with the panic as well. The next day when the social worker called, I saw the number and almost didn't answer. He was wearing me down, and I didn't want to risk giving in. It was the first time I said no and stuck to it. Unfortunately, the system failed, and he was back on the streets.

An advantage of going to jail for a drug-related charge is that Nevada has a drug court. These specialty courts are problem-solving court strategies designed to address the root causes of criminal activity and, in the case of adult drug courts, facilitate testing, treatment, and oversight. Gerad's disadvantage was twofold. He was arrested in Elko County, which didn't have specialty courts, and he had two arrests, and each case was assigned to two different judges. It had been a 50/50 shot since there were only two criminal judges in Elko County. He had to do everything twice and hoped to get not one but both judges to agree. We were trying to get him released to a long-term rehab, following the same rules as drug court, but he wasn't technically in drug court. And more importantly, Gerad had to agree to go. This was Elko County, not Washoe County, and the rules were not as familiar to our attorney. I looked up our county's drug court rules online and pitched the plan. If Gerad could complete a long-term program and stay clean for one year afterward, with regular testing, it would meet the requirements of other drug courts in the state. Of course, there were no long-term treatment facilities available in Nevada to those not enrolled in drug court. I figured I'd worry about that later, but most importantly, I had to make sure that Gerad would agree. Previously Gerad had balked at even a 90-day program, and I was asking him to go for a year. I told him about the idea, and he didn't hesitate, "I'll go. I can't do this anymore." By this time, I knew I couldn't be sure he was sincere or just hoping for a "get out of jail free" card. Like finding a long-term facility, I figured I'd cross that bridge when I got there.

Since there were no long-term programs in Nevada, I began calling some in California. Our attorney cautioned us that convincing two judges to let Gerad leave the state may be impossible. With the absence of these types of programs in Nevada, I felt we had a good chance to convince them if, and it was still a big if, they even bought into the drug court model. I googled long-term addiction programs in California and started calling. Most facilities defined long-term as 90 days with a move to a sober house for up to six months after completing the program. I wasn't even sure if this would suffice, but I had to try.

I had enrolled in COBRA for Gerad's health insurance from his job at the grocery store, which would up his chances of getting into treatment at a reputable facility. The first two places I called let me know that Gerad's insurance probably wouldn't cover his stay because he had to be in withdrawals to be considered high-risk. "The fact that he is in jail and technically sober won't meet the test of medical necessity," one admission counselor said. You would think I would be used to this kind of insanity, but this one hit hard. "He is in jail for possession of heroin," I said. "That isn't enough?" He apologized for the way the system worked, so I asked about the cost. It was $30,000 upfront for 30 days. A quick calculation told me I'd need $90,000 for 90 days. If he walked away on day two, there would be no refunds. At least they had a sober living community Gerad could live in after he completed the program. I told him I'd get the money.

The counselor, Brook, asked me to tell him about what was going on with Gerad, so I spent 30 minutes recapping his addiction history. He asked a few follow-up questions and seemed genuinely interested in getting more information. Then he asked me a strange question. "Can I call you after work this evening?" I figured it couldn't hurt, so I said sure but didn't really expect a call. He called. He told me Gerad's story reminded him a lot of his own story, a story he normally didn't share with clients or their families. Brook and Gerad were similar in age, had both attended college, had supportive families, and had been terrible addicts that relapsed multiple times trying to get clean. "I think you ought to send Gerad to where I got sober." He went on to tell me that there were only two truly long-term rehab programs in the country. His definition of long-term was one year as an inpatient with one year of aftercare. One was in New Jersey, and one was in Texas, where Brook was originally from. He said he was a tough case and ended up spending even longer than a year. "Burning Tree Ranch, it's the toughest thing Gerad will ever do, but I think it's his best shot at getting sober. I thought I was so smart and so charming, but those counselors have seen it all." He explained that only people who relapsed multiple times go to the Ranch. He gave me the phone number of their Director of Admissions, and I texted her immediately. By morning I had a response. She said she would email me some paperwork and explained that Gerad would have to have an assessment by their medical director. That dreaded word. "He's in jail," I explained. She asked if a call could be scheduled, and I said I'd find out but doubted it. She said she would find out if the assessment could be done by me. It was always two steps forward and one step back, even on a good day.

Scheduling the court hearings took much longer than anticipated, and Burning Tree checked in every couple of weeks to find out if we were any closer. The admissions counselor offered to write a letter outlining their program and an official acceptance. The assessment had to be done within 30 days of admission. We'd been here before. I crossed my fingers and hoped all the pieces would line up. Our attorney lived in Reno, so he was trying to get the court dates coordinated on one day. The drive was brutal, and it was proving impossible to find a date that worked for both judges. We played the waiting game once more.

Gerad's hearing date finally came in September 2018, and we took what we hoped was one last trip to Elko. The first hearing was located at the jail in the morning. It was a typical courtroom despite its location. The room was longer than it was wide, and the judge's bench presided high above the tables for the defense and prosecution. We could watch from a glassed-in room at the south end of the courtroom which was dark and made the courtroom seem extra bright. Defense attorneys from the first few cases joked and laughed with the prosecutors. Elko was a small town, and I figured they knew each other's families. They were dressed in a jacket and tie, no suits, and teased the court reporter as if they had been friends since high school. Our attorney was from the "big city" of Reno, and I was worried that his expensive suit would put the judge off. Too late now.

The Bailiff began to bring the first defendants in, and the judge soon followed. He was tall and gaunt with close-cropped hair and wore cowboy boots under his robe. He couldn't be any more stereotypical for a judge from rural Nevada. There were two cases in front of Gerad's, and both of those attorneys and their clients irritated the judge. He made it clear that he was unhappy and denied bail. Gerad came next. He was escorted into the courtroom in his orange jumpsuit and placed in a chair next to his attorney. He was looking around for us when he came in, but the lighting made it impossible to see us. I mouthed words of encouragement even though I knew he couldn't see me. Our attorney went over a brief history of Gerad's issues with substance abuse and explained our request to send him to long-term rehab. I had given him a letter from Burning Tree that explained his acceptance to the program, their process for dealing with the courts, and the requirements to complete the program. It took five minutes for this judge to agree to let Gerad try rehab, and he was supposed to be the tough one! Gerad stood and smiled and shook his attorney's hand, and then he was escorted back to his cell. One down, one to go.

The second hearing was supposed to start at 1:00 pm at the courthouse in downtown Elko. We decided to go for an early lunch, happy about our first success. As soon as we sat down, I got a call on my cell phone. It was Gerad. "Can you come get me?" he said. "Get you, where?" He explained that when he got back to his cell, the guard told him to pack up, he was being released. I turned to our attorney and asked if that sounded right. He said that he understood Gerad would stay in jail and be driven to the next hearing. I turned my attention back to the call. "Mom, I'm already outside the jail. "I left the table and drove back to the jail, and sure enough, Gerad was on a bench outside. He stood as I pulled up and came to the passenger side of the car with a small box. "I don't know what's going on, but get in," I told him.

We drove back to the restaurant, finished lunch, and headed to the courthouse. As in many old towns in the West, the courthouse sat in the middle of downtown. It was three stories high, brick and stone, with carved wooden doors at the end of large steps leading up to the front of the building. No one used that entrance anymore, so we headed to the side entrance where metal detectors and x-ray equipment had been installed. We arrived early and headed up the first flight of stairs to check that Gerad's name was on the schedule, but it was lunchtime, and no one was in their offices. We landed near the original entrance, which had a large carved staircase directly across from it. It was beautiful. The place was quiet, and it seemed we were the only ones in the building. When the prosecutor arrived, our attorney walked over to find out what was going on. They walked over to the judge's clerk to get clarification. When our attorney came back over, he said there had been a mistake, and Gerad was not supposed to have been released from jail. The second judge refused to hear his case because he had been out of jail and could pose a danger to the court. You just can't make this stuff up, I thought. The jail makes a mistake, and Gerad pays the price. I asked our attorney to please explain our situation to the judge. He walked back over to the clerk and requested a conference with the judge before court started. The prosecutor supported it, and the clerk went to talk to the judge. There are so many hills to die on in the addiction fight, and I didn't want this to be the final nail in Gerad's coffin.

The judge finally agreed to hear Gerad's case with a few precautions in place. He was searched and kept out of the courtroom until the proceedings began. We entered a courtroom from days gone by. The woodwork was beautifully carved and well-tended, and long velvet curtains hung at the windows. Someone appreciated the history of this place enough to preserve it. The courtroom was large, with just a few people scattered in the seats. Gerad's case was second this time, and he had walked in with his attorney and sat down. The judge entered, a female, and we all rose. The first case went fairly quickly. The judge was succinct and unmoved by the defendant's excuses. She did, however, release him since he had proof of a job and a place to live. I considered it a good sign. His girlfriend sobbed with relief. Gerad and his attorney moved up to the table. The prosecutor outlined the charges against Gerad. I had learned that much of the work of a trial is done between attorneys prior to the hearing. Gerad's attorney had numerous meetings and phone calls with the prosecutor to gain his support for our plan. We hoped the prosecutor's backing would sway the judge. Gerad's attorney rose and went through Gerad's history. He handed the letter from Burning Tree to the Bailiff, who handed it to the judge. The judge asked if Gerad had family in the courtroom, and the attorney pointed us out. She read the letter and asked, "Why Texas?" The attorney explained that it was one of the few long-term treatment facilities for cases like Gerad's. She asked several more questions that sounded skeptical and wary of our request, and she expressed concern for Gerad's chance to follow through. Gerad wasn't required to make a plea at this hearing since we were asking to defer until after he completed treatment. Finally, she said she was leaning toward granting the request with several stipulations; regular phone conferences with our attorney, monthly written updates from Burning Tree, and proof of negative drug tests. Also, I would be held responsible for getting him to Burning Tree immediately. "I release Mr. Davis into the custody of his parents, with the understanding they will take him to this facility immediately." She turned to Gerad and said, "I hope you know how lucky you are to have a family willing to pay to give you this chance. Good luck, Mr. Davis." The attorney turned around with a big grin on his face and raised his eyebrows. I exhaled. We were one step closer to giving Gerad a real chance. I just had to get him there.

We practically ran to the car just in case they changed their minds. We headed back to Reno, elated about one of our first victories in this fight. As we entered the highway, Gerad commented on how strange it was to go so fast. He hadn't been in a car in nearly five months. He kept saying how surreal it felt to be out. I saw a grin on his face for the first time in a long time. It wasn't long before my mind wandered to the task ahead. I hadn't bought airline tickets to Dallas yet since I was unsure what the outcome would be in court. I had told Burning Tree Gerad's hearing date and let them know he had been released as soon as we got in the car. I was still waiting to hear back about when he could be admitted. One of the advantages of the new facility being in Texas was that Gerad's older brother lived there. He was comforted by knowing someone would be close by. That was true when this latest ordeal happened, but in the ensuing months, Ryan had decided to leave the Army and come back to Reno. I hadn't told Gerad yet. Ryan's wife had been nice enough to drive the two hours from Killeen, Texas, to check Burning Tree out. I had become wary from Gerad's experience at the last facility in Elko. He had completed his thirty days, but it had been more of a holding facility: not much treatment or preparation for the outside world. She gave it two thumbs up, which I conveyed to Gerad. He seemed relieved.

Once we were back in Reno, I finalized the arrangements for our trip to Dallas. Gerad would have to hang on for seven days. Our attorney was concerned that we weren't leaving soon enough, and rightly so. Just because Gerad had been sober for five months didn't mean anything had changed for him. I kept him close, brought his daughter to stay with us, made him attend two weddings with me, and monitored him closely. He had previously described the panic he would go into right before an attempt to get clean. It included trying to score one last time. I had scoured all the personal things he had brought from Elko and the things I had picked up after his arrest. His brother had checked his truck which he and I had to retrieve in Elko after his second arrest. It had been impounded, and there was so much drug paraphernalia scattered throughout I was afraid we had missed something. Gerad told me later he had gone up to the truck multiple times, hoping to find something. Sleep was difficult as I counted down the days. Six more days, five more days, four more days, and maybe, just maybe, this will be over.

Chapter Eight

Incarceration: Gerad

"I wake up every day inside the jail of addiction."
Gerad Davis

Rock bottom may look different on the outside for every addict, but on the inside, we all come to the same realization; only help from something bigger than ourselves will solve the internal emptiness. The night I got arrested for the last time, I wasn't scared; I didn't want to cry or scream at the top of my lungs; instead, I was completely docile, like I had been tranquilized. Granted, I wasn't dope sick yet, but it felt different this time. One thing was certain; I knew being arrested while out on bail meant I was in deep shit now. My mind was suddenly incapable of coming up with any more manipulating things to tell my mom. I was going to be in jail for a while this time, and it was something I had to accept.

I'd never felt more powerless, and I had to swallow the truth about my situation. When you get to jail, they strip you down from head to toe like a stolen car at a chop shop. Any shred of dignity you have left disappears as they tell you to lift your sack, spread your cheeks, and cough three times. If you don't cough hard enough, they will make you do it again until they are satisfied. My clothes were traded for a pair of itchy pants and a shirt that felt just like canvas. "Property of Elko County" was written on all the seams and tags to remind you just how out of control your life has become. The whole getup was topped off with some neon orange crocs. "Looking good now, Mom, don't brag too much about me to all your friends."

After the transformation, I was placed in a holding cell with several other men sleeping off their bad choices. A wool blanket and a hardy helping of two pieces of white bread with a slice of Kraft Singles cheese were handed over, with no pillow to help me relax. All jails are made of concrete and cinderblock and kept at a balmy 60 degrees or less to make your stay as "comfortable" as possible. I slept on that concrete bench for at least 12 hours, waiting for them to put me in the general population. Elko County doesn't have a big jail by any means, so it's not like they're backed up with degenerates and can't shuffle people through. I kept imagining a room full of cops watching the cameras and laughing at all the guys puking and talking to themselves, struggling to sleep in the holding cell.

Minutes felt like hours. I resisted calling my mom this time because the thought of wasting her time and money yet again created insurmountable shame. All bets were off as soon as I felt the sickness coming on. I had to throw a Hail Mary if I wanted to get well. After you call your loved one a million times to bail you out or save you, there is a numbed-out tone to their voice when they speak. She had finally become ambivalent to my cries for help. It didn't take long to realize that she wasn't going to get me out of this one. No one could get me out.

After a week of sweating, aching, and not wanting to move, my senses came back to life. My ability to adjust and adapt to any situation has always been intriguing to me. One good thing about being an addict is the resourcefulness and resilience you develop to get through difficulty. It's adapt or die. My day-to-day life became a forced routine at the hands of an invisible puppet master. Cell Block D was my new home, filled with 11 strangers. They weren't shy about telling me to take a shower after I'd lay in my misery for a few days. This environment forces you to be aware of others and respect everyone's space equally. Therefore, if you are stinking up the pod by not showering, then you are disrespecting everyone that lives there.

A couple of weeks in, I saw two guys fight over a seat and control of the TV remote. One of them ended up in the hospital, getting stitches in his eye. When a fight happens, they lock everyone down in their cell. You spend 23 hours in there and get one hour to shower and call whoever you choose. This lasts as long as the puppet master wants it to. My survival skills of observing and being good at making friends came in very handy. I stayed as small as possible and tried my hardest not to ruffle any feathers. Guys would fight over things that seemed so trivial on the outside, and I wasn't trying to stay any longer than I had to. It was sad to see how many drug addicts were in jail with me, and I kept wondering where the system had failed. Drug addicts are repeat offenders because we never get the chance to sort out the root causes of our trauma and other issues. I kept using because I needed the effect produced by heroin, the utter blankness. It took a couple of months to really surrender and accept the reality that I wasn't getting out until I saw the judge in court. I talked to many inmates about how my case was bullshit and that the cops said they pulled me over for a broken taillight when it was working fine. All the jailhouse lawyers would agree with me and encourage me to fight it, and we would get riled up together like a bunch of apes planning to bust out of the zoo. It was nonsense, but it helped pass the time.

There were a couple of key moments that stuck out to me during this time. I called my mom almost every day because it was comforting to hear her voice. We would talk about what my plan was after I got out of jail, and for the first time, I had no answer for her. We talked about treatment and sober living, and I clearly recall telling her, "Mom, I'm tired of trying to figure out what to do. Whatever you think I should do, I'm going to do." This was the first time in my life I completely surrendered to someone else's idea of what was best for me. She suggested a long-term treatment center, and I assured her I was open to whatever she thought was best. I was clearly incapable of getting myself out of shit since the harder I tried, the worse it got. Once I committed to doing whatever it took, I knew I still had months in jail to think about it, but my mind never changed about long-term treatment. It's a miracle for any addict to follow through with anything.

When a new inmate arrived in my pod, he proceeded to tell us that he had swallowed a bunch of meth and heroin and had it sitting in his stomach for several days. The interesting part was that he also smuggled some tobacco and a lighter in his ass. My addict brain took over, and I remember thinking, "Jesus, why wouldn't you put the drugs up your butt? Screw the tobacco!" I made friends with this guy, and we smoked his "booty" tobacco. He told me he would share the drugs if I helped him get them out. For several days he chugged water, drank Visine, and shoved his fingers down his throat. Nothing was working. Even though I was four months sober at this point, I knew if I got a hold of those drugs, I wouldn't hesitate to take them. On the last night he was there, there were three of us huddled in the bathroom area, watching him puke and then digging through the toilet to see if any treasures had come out. Suddenly, he was way too high to even function. I snapped out of my obsessive search and said, "Holy shit, he's going to overdose!"

The problem with swallowing a lot of meth and heroin concealed in Ziplock bags is that your stomach acid will eventually eat through the plastic. The bags began to open in his stomach, and the situation became life or death within seconds. We argued about who was going to tell the guard because in jail, the less involved you are, the better. Another inmate and I dragged him across to the door and called for help. The guards came in and asked what the hell was going on, but they figured it out quickly. I assume this isn't a new occurrence in jails. They called an ambulance, and care flighted him to Salt Lake City. I never saw him again. It's hard to say what happened to him or if he made it to the hospital alive. That experience showed me how selfish and disgusting of a person I could be. I was so focused on getting high that I failed to see another human being's life was at stake; a person with a mother and a family that cared about him. I couldn't help but think how tragic that would have been for my family. I could have easily been the guy smuggling drugs into jail. Looking back on that experience, I can see that something powerful was directing me down the right path. If I had gotten high with that guy, my story might have had a very different ending.

The last month slowly crawled by as I awaited my court appearance. I kept my head down and read veraciously to avoid any situations like that happening again. When the day finally came to go to court, I was terrified. I had two appearances in front of two separate judges and had to convince them both to release me to go to treatment in Texas. It seemed like a long shot. The worst part about waiting in jail for five months was the unknown. My fate was in the hands of others. I had no idea if I was going to be released or be sentenced to prison. My life's direction rested with not one but two judges.

The first court appearance was at the jail. Most county jails have found it safer and easier to have a courtroom on-site to avoid any mishaps. On court days, the guards go around to every pod at 7 am and call out the names of those going that day. I was added to the convict train with shackles and handcuffs. As we moved toward the courtroom, they added several other inmates, and then we were all placed in a white room with cinder block walls and cement benches. I recognized three of the eight people in the room from the streets of Elko. Small town. It became obvious that people with drug problems were prime targets for the local police.

I was worried about seeing the first judge because I heard he was a hard ass from other inmates. When it was my turn to go, I was escorted in and immediately scanned the room, looking for my mom. There was a mirrored glass wall in the back of the courtroom, and I knew my mom was behind it. It was comforting to know she was there. She never gave up on me, and I was hoping for both of us that this was going to be a turn in the right direction. I sat next to my lawyer and eagerly listened to what the judge thought of our plan. Was it too crazy? Were they really going to let me leave the state to go to treatment? My mom later told me that the judge had cowboy boots under his robe, and I smiled, imagining six shooters on his hip too. He was surprisingly sympathetic to my situation and quickly agreed to release me. I was floored. It was too good to be true! "One down, one to go," my lawyer said as I thanked him and exited with the guard to head back to M block.

I was feeling hopeful and encouraged as I told my fellow cell-mates what had happened. Suddenly, a guard came in and yelled, "Davis, roll it up!" These are the words that every inmate waits to hear. It means that you are being released. My understanding was that I would have to see both judges before they would release me, so I hesitated. The guard yelled, "Hurry up before I change my mind." I wasn't hesitating this time. I quickly jumped up from the table and threw my belongings on my mattress and rolled it up like a burrito. I quickly said my goodbyes to the few that I was close with and ran out the door. "What the hell was happening?" I thought to myself. I wasn't about to ask questions. The guard asked me how long I had been in there, and I told him five months. He gasped and said, "Really, damn, I wonder why it took so long to see a judge." Yeah, you and me both, buddy.

I filled out some paperwork and changed into the clothes that I got arrested in. The clothes are always rancid when you get them back; it wasn't like I was staying at the Marriott with laundry and turndown service. I was grateful to be leaving. I immediately called my mom when I got outside, and she was just as shocked as I was. Somebody messed up somewhere, and I scanned my surroundings, waiting for an officer to pop up and tackle me. I sat down on a bright blue metal bench and drifted into silent revelations. I felt the sun on my skin for the first time in five months and realized how pale my skin had become behind closed doors. I was paralyzed with thoughts and questions and sat there waiting for a nudge in any direction. I would have sat there for hours if my mom didn't pick me up. I didn't know what to do with myself.

I jumped in the car and proceeded to meet my lawyer and stepdad for lunch. Everything felt surreal and took some adjusting. Eating real food didn't make sense, and I realized all the small things I had taken for granted. The common staples of life are easily forgotten when you're forced to adhere to a different set of rules, things like time, food, and going where you want when you want. We finished lunch and headed to the courthouse to see the second judge. She was supposed to be the easy one, but things unexpectedly unfolded when we arrived. The judge refused to see me for security reasons since I had been released from jail with no supervision. Somewhere a miscommunication occurred between my first court appearance and the courthouse I was currently in. I couldn't believe that I had waited five months to get shafted. My lawyer sprang into action and met with the judge before the hearing started and somehow got the District Attorney and judge to agree to see me. Having a charismatic lawyer paid off in moments like these.

We were escorted into the courtroom, and it felt like I was transported into an old Western movie. Unlike the jail courthouse, this room was large and had carved wood trim on everything. Every move someone made created a creaking sound, from walking on the floor to sitting on the bench. It was clear that this place was at least 100 years old and very well-kept. The judges' bench was far above everyone and everything else in the room, and that position worked well for intimidating the shit out of me. I was called second, and my lawyer pleaded the same case, requesting that they consider releasing me to go to long-term treatment. It was hard to read the judge's facial expressions, but I figured years of hearing cases like mine had to eventually make you numb. She was satisfied with the terms if I was subjected to regular drug testing, and I went to the treatment facility immediately. She released me to the custody of my mom and stepdad, and I felt a wave of hope rush over me for the first time in years. Maybe I do have a chance.

I rode back to Reno with my mom, and we celebrated what felt like the first small victory. I remember telling her I really wanted to stop and get some cigarettes, and she said, "Why would you want to do that? You haven't smoked in five months." What I didn't know back then that I do know now, was I was trying to change the way that I felt by any means necessary. All the restlessness and irritability were coming out in full force, and I didn't have any clue how to deal with those feelings in a healthy way. The obsession was on me like a gorilla. I thought about how I would change that during the four-hour car ride home to Reno.

I waited a week before flying to Texas. If I told you that it was easy, I would be lying. I researched Burning Tree Ranch relentlessly and watched all the alumni videos that were available. Their marketing game was strong enough to convince me that I was making the right decision. As the week dragged on, I became more fearful and angrier about the whole process. It was hard to sleep at night, and I was unable to be present for my family and Tatum. I kept thinking about how unfair it was that I was a drug addict and had to go to long-term treatment just to live. I wasn't going to college or getting any sort of certificate; I was trying not to die or have felonies on my record, that's it. Those are things that normal people never have to consider. The victim mentality was hard to crawl my way out of, and all these thoughts became so obsessive that I started looking for anything to soothe the torment that I was experiencing. I rummaged through my 4Runner several times that week, looking for any scraps of heroin or meth that might have been overlooked when my brother and mother cleaned it out. I even went as far as cutting the carpets open and looking in all the cracks and crevasses. If I had the tools, I would have taken the damn seats out. I wasn't going to stop until I found a morsel of comfort to shut off this nagging itch.

My only treasure from that hunt was a few loose cigarette butts from the ashtray, which I took and emptied out into a rolling paper and smoked. It gave me a head rush, and the relief I felt from those 30 seconds was so profound that I had a moment of clarity. I realized that I was digging through my 4Runner like a dope fiend who had been up for weeks on end. The big difference was that I was five months sober at this point, and there were no drugs in my system, so why was I behaving this way? For the first time, it dawned on me that I was out of my league and there were bigger things at play that I didn't understand. I wanted relief from this prison, and I needed to ask for help from someone who had the key.

Chapter Nine

The Ranch: Lisa

"Sometimes the bravest and most
important thing you can do is just show up."
Brené Brown

A s I was standing in the back of the room watching a teary-eyed speech from a grateful father, I felt hopeful. It was graduation day at Burning Tree Ranch, and three women had successfully completed two years of treatment. Staff recalled funny stories about them, and the women teased the staff, recalling the escapades where they thought they had outsmarted them. They were glowing, happy, and excited for their future. All the things Gerad was not. This graduation ceremony happened to be during alumni weekend. Just the fact that they had an alumni weekend was encouraging. Many ex-clients were enjoying a BBQ and catching up with old friends. The Ranch attracts stray dogs from all over the area, and it was amazing how attached the clients had become to them. People were often more excited to see old friends of the four-legged variety. I guess they'd all felt like strays, too, seeking shelter where all were welcome.

It was early October 2018, and my first visitation since Gerad arrived. Through a weird timing of events, I would see Gerad three times in his first two months; alumni weekend, post-admission intervention, and the first regularly scheduled visitation. I believe I had been invited to alumni weekend by mistake since it happened to fall before the required family orientation, a prerequisite for visitation. We went in with little guidance, so we had no idea what to expect. Gerad's older brother came too. I remember watching the ceremony with a sense of relief. Gerad was in the right place, and in two short years, I would be standing here again and celebrating his success. I was sure of it.

I had dropped Gerad off in September, a week after he had been released from jail. It had been a long week trying to keep him busy and prepare for what would be a long stay in treatment. He had to have a negative drug test when he arrived, so I watched him like a hawk. We had been given a very specific packing list and the do's and don'ts of life at The Ranch. His daughter stayed with us for a few days as he prepared to leave. We all had a different energy. Mine was hopeful and happy the chips had all fallen into place; Gerad was nervous and quiet, and his daughter was unsure what this trip meant but was content to spend time with her dad. When our departure day finally came, and with two large suitcases packed, we headed to the airport. After a long plane ride and a one-and-a-half-hour drive from Dallas, we began to see signs directing us to The Ranch. Gerad had grown quiet once we turned off the Interstate onto a narrow country road that would take us down the last few miles of our trip. He had been fiddling around with an iPod, trying to get the music to download. I asked him if he was ready. "I'm nervous." He fidgeted and looked out the window as we pulled up to the gate.

I had been instructed to stop at the admissions building located inside the entrance, where the intake process would begin. I found out later it sat where the first structure at The Ranch existed and where the founder lived as he built the place. We walked up to the attached wooden porch and opened the door to a blast of air conditioning. We entered the largest of what looked like two rooms. After introductions, we were directed down a long narrow hall to an office with a desk, filing cabinet, and two chairs. As I looked around, the women in the office joked and laughed putting us at ease. I handed over Gerad's ID, insurance card, and a cashier's check that would cover the first three months of his stay. She had him take a seat as I stood in the doorway while she entered his information into the computer.

Within a few minutes, the "buddy" Gerad had been assigned walked into the office. His name was Jay, but he said everyone called him "Coach." Gerad would stick close to him for the first few days to learn the schedule and expectations of ranch life. Since the office was crowded, I moved outside and waited to take a quick tour. Considering how long it had taken us to get to this point in our journey, I was at The Ranch for a relatively short period of time before heading back.

One of the counselors and the Director gave me my tour. Both were recovering alcoholics and drug addicts, and they listened with empathy as I told them a bit about Gerad, and they told me a bit about themselves. The Director had been in recovery with the founder of The Ranch, David Elliott, and had been asked to run The Ranch a few years before. The tour didn't take long. Besides the admissions building, there were only four other structures. The main house, with the large meeting area and women's dorm, was Spanish style, with a large pond and garden behind it. An in-ground swimming pool was off to the side of the house. The land surrounding The Ranch was flat and green, taking your eye to the horizon far beyond where thick rows of trees divided property lines. There was no similarity or continuity between the buildings. Each was built at a different time and for different uses. I wondered if the founder had ever envisioned the growth The Ranch would have beyond that original structure. They showed me where Gerad would probably be living. It was a small house with a large yard out front. It had a central living area with dorm-style rooms around it. I noticed a guitar out on the couch and mentioned Gerad liked to play. I hoped it made him feel more comfortable. The men's and women's quarters were separated, but all came together in the other buildings, where meetings and group sessions occurred. We walked through what looked like the newest building; it was full of tables and chairs and was where all the meals were taken. It had tall windows, was full of light, and had stairs leading to offices on the second floor. Clients weren't served meals but were expected to prepare their own, as well as prepare meals for each other. It was an impressive kitchen, and large-scale paintings by the founder's favorite artist hung on the wall.

David had purchased The Ranch after getting sober and decided that building a long-term recovery center was his life's purpose. He had recovered at a similar facility in Arizona, but it had closed after the woman that ran it retired. There was only one such place left at the time in New Jersey. Seeing him speak at graduation and then family orientation a few months later, I quickly understood that he was a no-nonsense guy who spoke of the stark realities of addiction. He pulled no punches when he spoke of the manipulation and selfishness of addicts. It was startling but also reassuring. Gerad couldn't hide here. He would be held accountable and required to put it all out there. He was in good company as many of the staff were in recovery. There is no one better to see through the bullshit of an addict than an addict in recovery.

I went back to admissions to say goodbye. Gerad looked up as I entered the room; he was terrified. I hugged him tight and left before I changed my mind. It would be a long haul. The program required a year-long residential stay at The Ranch, six months in a sober living house, and another six months in an apartment. It was two years in total. No wonder he was terrified. The longest he had ever been in treatment was 30 days. The Director told me that many people dropped off their loved ones and left immediately. They can't get away fast enough.

The last time I felt this mix of fear and excitement, I was dropping Gerad off at the airport as he headed to a skateboard camp in Oregon. It was the summer before his senior year in high school. He had never gone anywhere on his own, and I could tell he was nervous about navigating the airports and finding the camp director when he landed. I was just as nervous but assured him everything would be fine and he would have a great time. I bought him a special backpack that held his skateboard so he could carry it on the plane. That's the image I think of when I remember that trip; Gerad walking to security, both hands on the straps of that "Skatepack," the wheels bouncing against his legs. He would be gone for two weeks, much longer than he had ever been away from home. I was excited about the possibilities the trip could bring and desperate for it to go well. Now, Gerad was facing two years away from everything he knew, good and bad. This time the trip was life or death.

Once back home, the sense that I could breathe returned. After so much time worrying about what the next phone call could bring, a break seems almost surreal. I was anxious to know how he was doing. His counselor made regular calls to update me on his progress, but it wasn't the same as seeing for myself. Visitation was allowed every other month for four hours. Phone calls were every Sunday for five minutes.

I was excited to go see Gerad but was unsure how he would react. Ryan and I followed the same winding country road and arrived 30 minutes before the scheduled visitation. As we approached the entrance, we saw cars lined up along the road. The families were expected to follow the rules as well, and the gate didn't open until noon. If you were late, you were turned away. We were directed by clients, strung along the road, to a parking lot behind the new building I had toured when I dropped Gerad off. I could see all the clients through the window, anxiously looking for their support system. We checked in outside and received a name badge. I was able to meet Beth, the admissions counselor that had walked me through the admission process months earlier and who had provided the letters for the court to get Gerad here. I hugged her and thanked her again for all her help.

I felt nervous as I approached the door. I wasn't sure what Gerad's reaction would be; angry for leaving him here or relieved I showed up. When I first broached going to Texas to a program, Gerad was more receptive because his older brother was stationed there. He had told me many times he didn't want to go somewhere he didn't know anyone. At the time, I couldn't be sure if it was another excuse not to seek treatment or a legitimate fear. Seeing his face through the glass, anxious, happy, and expectant, I knew family support was critical to him.

He gave me a big hug with a "Hi, Mom." He looked good but still pale and unsure. The Clinical Director talked to us about the importance of keeping things simple, "News, weather, and sports." We were asked not to share photos on our phones or give the client anything and were instructed to find a staff member if the client began asking to leave or discuss other topics. We weren't allowed to take photos, and where we could go was restricted to a few buildings and some of the grounds. I had no idea what Gerad's state of mind was, so I was worried about what we would have to discuss. I was glad Ryan had come with me.

He seemed genuinely happy to see us, and I was relieved to see him. There were some awkward silences, but for the most part, we were able to keep the conversation flowing. It was an adjustment on both sides, conversations with Gerad when he was sober. He showed us around and introduced us to his roommates. He said he was slowly adjusting. They stayed busy all day and were expected to wake up early, meditate, then complete their assigned chores. His task was cutting the grass. He asked if I could send him a watch since being late had consequences he would rather avoid. He also needed collared shirts and khakis to follow the dress code for meetings. Because it was alumni weekend, they were having a BBQ followed by a fireworks display. The clients appreciated talking to those alumni that had made it through and were living productive lives. Hope was in the air.

My next trip to Dallas, just a few weeks later, was at the request of the clinical staff at The Ranch. They believed it was important to bring the family down unexpectedly and tell the client the effect their addiction had on them, and most importantly, to set boundaries if the client chose to leave the program. They called it a post-admission intervention. Alec, Gerad's younger brother, came with me this time. He had watched Gerad deteriorate into the depths of addiction and had lost him, or at least who he thought his brother was, in the process.

Upon arrival, we were greeted by Gerad's counselor and the head of the clinical program. They outlined what they hoped to accomplish during the session, let us know that Gerad did not know we were there, and then asked us to go over what we thought we would say. I had the same speech I had given Gerad many times, although I was nervous since finality was expected, but for Alec, this was new. He had never talked to his brother about the effect his addiction had on him. He became agitated and angry. He worried he wouldn't be able to control his anger when he talked to Gerad. He wanted to be anywhere other than this room, about to confront his brother about his feelings. He was brutally honest, and when asked what he wanted to say to Gerad, he replied, "I just want to beat the addiction out of him." He cried and became exasperated as he seemed to be trying to talk them out of having him confront Gerad. They were patient and calm and let him express his anger, fear, and disappointment. He had looked up to Gerad, and his fall was very painful for him to watch.

They both asked us if we were ready and then left to get Gerad. Alec was staring down at the table, tears still in his eyes from the emotional retelling of his devastation at Gerad's downfall. I kept a calm demeanor for him but could feel the butterflies begin to flutter, and my heart raced as the door opened and Gerad stepped into the room. He was surprised and a bit shell-shocked to see us, especially Alec. He hesitantly sat down, and the team explained to him what was going on. All the clients knew this would happen at some point, but they were never told when it would be scheduled.

I went first and told Gerad I couldn't watch him die. He had to make it through this program and stay sober, or he was no longer welcome back into our family. He stayed quiet and looked pale and anxious. I had given this speech to Gerad before, but I had never said never.

Alec went next and did an amazing job. He told Gerad how he had always looked up to him and that he thought he was the coolest person he had ever met. He said, "You had it all, could do anything, be anything, you're better than this."

Tears began to stream down Gerad's face. Alec was wired but determined. I have never been prouder of him. The whole thing only lasted 10 minutes. Gerad stood, and we both hugged him, and then he was whisked away. The counselors let Alec know what a phenomenal job he had done, and we headed back to the airport emotionally spent.

I had somehow skirted the required family orientation early on but was asked to attend prior to any more visitations. So once again, for the third time in two months, I hopped on a plane and made my way to Dallas. I found The Ranch Aftercare Office in Dallas, headed upstairs, and sat at my assigned table with another family. The staff went over the program and the rules put in place for the clients and their families to give the addict the best chance at recovery. I sat back and watched the various family dynamics unfold. A young wife wanted to know what to tell her neighbors when they asked where her husband had gone. Her co-dependency was written in her body language and her quivering lip. A wife, here with her two sons, was angry that she now had to go back to work and raise two boys by herself for the next two years. In both cases, I was sure neither husband would make it to sobriety. I felt judgmental and sad, I didn't know what they had been through, but I did know that unless you could get out of your own misery and focus on what the addict did and didn't need from you, treatment would fail.

Getting past your own pain is easier said than done, believe me, but understanding the depth of the pain Gerad was in was even more heartbreaking, gut-wrenching, sickening, and exasperating. I also knew The Ranch was the last resort in many aspects, and I needed to let the experts guide me. I paid attention to the counselor, who asked us to be a partner with them, to the addict, and the pitfalls encountered as they worked on finishing the program and the guided aftercare program. They described a multi-disciplinary approach rooted in the twelve steps, including private psychotherapy sessions, group therapy, EMDR (Eye Movement Desensitization and Reprocessing), and nutritional and exercise guidance. I focused on their advice, what to talk about and what not to talk about when visiting, and what Gerad would need from me through this process. I was aiming for a grade of A+ as mother-of-a-client. I knew it was Gerad's best chance, his only chance.

Chapter Nine

The Ranch: Gerad

"Your hardest times
often lead to the greatest
moments of your life."
Roy T. Bennett

The day had come to travel to Texas, and I feared what was to come. We received an email with a packing list and a description of all the restrictions that had to be followed upon admission to The Ranch. There were so many rules and regulations that I questioned if I was making a huge mistake. There was a constant voice in my head, always trying to convince me that I was overreacting and that I didn't need this kind of help. I would go back and forth, persuading myself I needed this but also why I should run away.

I wasn't aware of what the length of my stay would be until I got to The Ranch. They kept that information quiet because if an addict like me heard that it was a year-long inpatient program with another year of aftercare, I would never have made it there. Time is a hard sell for people looking for a quick fix for all their problems. A bit of good news; I could have music if it was on a device that wasn't connected to the internet. What is this, 2008? Everything was connected these days, and it was challenging to track down an old iPod Nano off Craigslist. The actual transaction reminded me of the drug deals I did in parking lots. We set a meeting place at a random grocery store in Reno, and my mom gave me the cash to jump into a stranger's car and get the goods. I kept thinking, "This is oddly similar to scoring drugs, except the guy actually showed up on time and had exactly what I asked for." My mom wanted to see what I had bought when I got back in the car. I didn't take offense because I was as shady as the day was long. I proudly showed her, like a kindergarten kid showing one of his finger paintings from school. I was doing the right thing for once in a sea of mistakes and lies. I distracted myself with that iPod during the entire drive to The Ranch and was still working on it as we pulled up to the admissions building. I was terrified.

As the drive progressed, I occasionally glanced out the car window. I sensed we were getting closer once we turned off the main highway. On both sides were occasional houses surrounded by large plots of land. We passed a sign that said, "Burning Tree Cattle Ranch," and my heart stopped. For a split second, I thought I signed up to be a ranch hand without knowing it. I wanted to jump out of the car in the middle of nowhere Texas and run anywhere but there. My anxiety was so high that it was hard to hear anything. The fight or flight response was welling up in me, and I wanted to abort the mission.

We arrived at a big red metal gate, and my mom pushed the button on the intercom to announce our arrival. On the right was not just the admissions building but also the administrative offices. The surroundings looked like a farm. There were a couple of older-looking horses grazing in the field. They looked peaceful, far more peaceful than I was feeling. We got out of the car and lugged my suitcases inside. I met a lot of people rapidly and was directed to a back room. They wanted to search all my belongings and give me a drug test immediately. Drug addicts can say a lot of things, but you can't hide from the facts of your behavior. The lady doing my admission told me it was procedure to search everything for the safety of the community. I obliged, but when it came to the drug test, I thought back to me scrummaging through my 4Runner, looking for drugs. The only thing I found were cigarette butts, but the ashtray smelled like weed, and I was worried that I might fail the drug test. Honestly, I was hoping that I would get kicked out before this nightmare began. It didn't matter that my mom flew all the way out to Texas and escorted me the whole way; it didn't matter that I had a prison sentence hanging over my head; all that mattered was not wanting to feel so uncomfortable. I passed the drug test and inspection, and we continued the paperwork. Once finished, she called and requested "Gerad's buddy" to be sent to admissions. He was about 50 years old, his hair was salt and pepper grey, and thankfully he had a great sense of humor that had me laughing within the first five minutes of meeting him. It was hard to believe that he was a client here. He was cheerful and full of life, and I was interested in how he could feel that way being in long-term treatment. My mom popped in to give me a hug and left before either of us could turn back. She wished me luck, and just like that, I was shoved in a different direction. I really wanted this to be the end of a long battle, and I had hope in my heart for the first time in years.

The Ranch was a 33-acre plot of land in the middle of nowhere. It had lush green vegetation and a large pond in the middle of the property. The long driveway we had entered was lined with trees and continued past admission to a set of buildings where all the clients stayed. The main house was to the left as we walked by, and I was told that it was where most "groups" were held. We kept walking straight past a stucco-covered two-story building where I would be staying. My buddy informed me that everyone was in group, and he was going to help me set up my room first, and then he would introduce me to everyone. The room was dorm-style, with two sets of bunk beds on opposite walls. There were a couple of dressers that had seen better days, and random inspirational quotes hung in various places on the walls. I noticed blue books titled "Alcoholics Anonymous," which didn't help ease the doubts in my mind about the whole experience. This was my first "big boy" rehab, and I expected to be pampered and catered to because that was what I heard and read about 99% of rehabs. I quickly learned that this place was not like most rehabs. There was a strict schedule to be kept, and the clients were required to prepare all meals and clean on a regular basis. Everyone must be on shadow and boundary when they first arrive. Shadow means you must be within 10 feet of another client for the first week. Boundary meant you could have no interaction with the opposite sex. It felt childish and ridiculous, but I learned later how effective it was at showing the treatment team whether you were going to follow the rules or not. I wanted to do my best to adhere to the rules and show them that I wanted to be there and have a new life.

Everyone woke up early and prayed and meditated together as a group. This was my first hurdle. I had no experience with God or prayer, let alone meditation. So, I would sit there with my arms crossed and think how stupid this cult shit was to me. I thought I was open to new ideas and experiences, but this quickly showed me that I was far from surrendering my old beliefs and assumptions. Turns out prayer was a lot less foreign to me than my next hurdle, confrontations. The clients were expected to hold each other accountable and would confront each other every morning in a group called community. When a client needed to confront another client, they would say, "When you (blank), I feel (blank)." This group met in the main house in a giant room with a massive brick fireplace that had this ridiculous stuffed bull's head mounted above it. I would often stare at that bull during group. It was hard not to avoid. Every client and a few varied staff would attend. The chairs were set up in a perfect circle so we could all face each other. To me, it felt like a battlefield for the first few months. Staff and clients would confront and talk about issues that were coming up. This group happened five days a week, and most clients, including myself, would have great anxiety as it approached. I was never held accountable for my actions, so it was extremely uncomfortable to have things pointed out that were concerning. I thought treatment would be easier than jail, but boy, was I wrong.

During the next few months, I adjusted to getting up at 6 am and doing chores for an hour and a half, followed by group sessions all day. It's amazing what humans can adjust to in life, whether it's being homeless on the streets or being in treatment for a year. I slowly but surely started to change my thinking and outlook on life, mainly due to my introduction to the "big book" of Alcoholics Anonymous and the structure of working the 12 steps. There were other modes of therapy that coincided with getting me to a place of serenity and peace, but the change happened when I learned about the importance of connecting to a power greater than myself. If you make the connection, you have tools to solve problems, not just heroin, but anything that comes up in life. This all sounded good to me in theory, but I had a big issue with this "higher power" business. I couldn't wrap my head around what "God" was supposed to look like or what he could do for me. I really struggled to try to find some footing. Thankfully there is access to people with experience and struggles that match yours within the program. The treatment team told me to get a sponsor and helped me find one. A sponsor is someone who has worked the 12 steps and can mentor you through the process of getting connected. This was a necessary step for me to have any chance of success. If I learned anything up to this point, I knew that whatever I was trying before would always fail. There was no amount of willpower and self-help that was going to get me out of the grips of heroin.

The regular routines were interrupted only by visitation and graduations. The first graduation I saw there was inspiring. Not only did family attend, but I loved the fact that they had alumni and people in aftercare in attendance. They would come out to The Ranch often to inspire us. It was reassuring to hear the struggles and hurdles that people had overcome being new to sobriety. I watched in awe, thinking, "Wow, if I could make it to two years sober, that would be a miracle." I had a hard enough time putting together two days sober. The program taught me to focus on today, and that's what I did. It made the struggle a lot more manageable.

The treatment team was good at stripping away everything that I used as a crutch to really focus on the underlying issues that led me to this point. There were so many rules and restrictions I didn't understand, but they asked me to do them anyways. Things like five-minute phone calls every Sunday to family. No exceptions. I would always call my mom. She was always there, and I knew I could count on hearing her voice every week. The calls were short and sweet, but I would give her updates on my progress, and she would quickly update me on everyone in the family. We adjusted to this just like we adjusted to everything, good or bad.

The hardest rule required me to tell my daughter exactly what was going on to have her come to visitation. I was encouraged by my counselor to call her and explain where she would be coming to see me. The mind can be such a powerful place; it was insane the fear that I felt and the lies that I told myself. What if she never wants to talk to me again? What if she doesn't love me anymore? The manufactured fear can feel so real, and if I didn't have the support around me, I would have never followed through with it. I built up that conversation in my head for weeks, and when it finally happened, it was such a relief. My counselor sat with me as I called her, and Tatum was completely unphased by it. I told her that I was a drug addict and that I was in Texas getting some help at a facility. Without missing a beat, she said, "Okay, Daddy, I love you. I can't wait to see you!" My heart melted. She was more resilient than I gave her credit for. I felt unconditional love at that moment, and I was excited to build honest relationships with all my family members. I asked her to think of some questions for me and write them down to share when she came to visit. She said she would, but I wasn't sure what to expect.

Visitation happened every couple of months. As it happened, I saw my mom three times in the first two months after admission, two were good, and one was difficult. They have an alumni party which coincides with visitation every October with fireworks and catered food. It was nice to hear the success stories and see people that made it through the program and were living normal lives. Although I was supposed to be on a 30-day blackout from seeing any family, they invited everyone, and I was able to see my mom and my big brother within the first three weeks. I wasn't expecting it the second time.

Every client is subjected to a P.A.I. (post-admission intervention). They don't tell you when it's happening; they just randomly pull you from whatever you're doing and bring you to sit down in front of your family and hear what their boundaries are and what they are going to do if you leave treatment. My mom and brother were waiting for me when my turn came, and I sat down to hear them out. This was the first time I heard my mom say that she wasn't willing to help me anymore if I left treatment, which was difficult to hear. But what was the most heart-wrenching was facing my little brother as he poured his heart out. He said he wished he could beat the addiction out of me, and I couldn't agree more. I would have let him do it at that moment to take away his pain and tears. Something about that conversation really drove home the damage I had caused my family. When I was in the middle of using, I never considered the toll it was taking on the people closest to me. As hard as it was to hear, it was the truth, and I saw the importance of hearing it.

The third time was a regular visitation, and my mom brought Tatum, who was now nine. I was so nervous to see my daughter and kept imagining the questions she might have for me. It's an odd feeling being in treatment and having your child come to see you. I felt like a child in a fragile state, trying desperately to get better. I wanted her to see me as a hero, not a failure. I reminded myself that I had failed her a million times because of my addiction. I was an absent father for several years, but it wasn't because I didn't love her. I was caught in the grips of heroin, and that became my number one priority. Getting high and staying "well" was life or death, and it was the only thing that mattered for a long time.

The day she came, I was anxious, pacing back and forth, wondering if she would love me the same now that she knew what was

165

going on. I wanted her to be proud of me and know that I thought about her often. When she walked in the door, she ran up to me and gave me the biggest hug. I squeezed and held on a little longer than I probably should have. She was energetic and lively and wanted to meet all the dogs on the property. I walked with her everywhere and watched her do cartwheels and make friends with some of the other kids that were visiting. She was as happy and vivacious as I remembered, and I stalled having a serious talk with her for as long as possible. Visitation was only for four hours, so I had to pull her aside before it was too late. I was anxious to hear if she had come up with any questions. We sat next to each other, facing the giant pond with a loud water feature in the middle of it. You could hear it anywhere on the property. I hesitated to talk and finally asked her, "What do you think of this place?"

"It's beautiful! I love the dogs," she quickly replied.

"Did you think about our conversation? Do you have any questions for me?"

"Yes," she stared at the pond for a second, and I could see the wheels turning in her head.

"It's okay, babe. You can ask me anything you want. I want to answer whatever questions you might have."

Then, like a dam breaking open, she asked me three questions, laying them out in one breath.

"Why did you miss my last few birthdays? How long are you going to be here? Did you stop coming around because I did something wrong?

I was shocked, not because she had questions, but because she had obviously been thinking about these things for a long time. The last question was the one I had been most afraid she would ask. I explained to her that I was sick, like somebody with cancer. I was here in Texas getting treatment to deal with the things that happened in my life and get some healthy coping mechanisms. I continued and told her that I have and will always love her, then I burst into tears. I couldn't contain the shame and guilt that I felt for letting her down.

She instantly put her hand on my leg and softly said, "It's okay, Daddy. I love you too. I just want you to get better."

At this moment, with the sun starting to set in the sky and Tatum's hand on my leg, I knew things were changing. Pain is the touchstone to change, and being completely honest with my daughter was a cathartic experience.

Chapter Ten

Transformation: Lisa

"I have but one wish for you
And that is that you walk forward and leave it littered
With all the things that you were never meant to carry."
Jonathon Muncy Storm

The following year, 2019, became a routine of Sunday night phone calls, Thursday counseling updates from Keyana, visits to Dallas, and glimmers of hope. I looked forward to the Sunday calls and made sure I was always available at 7 pm. I was the only one on Gerad's approved call list, and there was a strict five-minute time limit, so I felt the importance of making the most of the time to keep him up to date with the family and the world. There was nothing unpleasant allowed, but I did occasionally mention an overdose death of someone one of us knew. I hoped it would help to reinforce how lucky he was to be alive and how important it was to keep working hard. Gerad would keep me updated on his progress through the 12 steps, explain shutdowns and when they happened, and recount trips when they were taken off The Ranch to attend the State Fair, a movie, or participate in community service at a senior center.

Shutdowns occurred when the community wasn't "showing up." There is a suspension of the regular daily clinical schedule. In its place, the entire clinical team co-facilitates a community-wide therapeutic group designed to address the ineffective behaviors/

belief system that are blocking progress. Accountability wasn't just about yourself but about holding others accountable. Clients could also receive a therapeutic intervention (TI) when they weren't being accountable or following the rules. They could last days or weeks and were assigned by their group counselor. Gerad received two, one for using sarcasm and one for rescuing other clients instead of holding them accountable. It was hard for Gerad to have the light shined directly on him. He preferred to sit back and lay low. He would tell me about his newest assigned buddy, who left the program and was getting ready to graduate. Because it was a small group of clients, around 25, you became familiar with them during visitation and cheered their successes and mourned their failures.

Before Gerad's daughter could visit him, he had to tell her the truth. Since I had always made excuses for her father's absence, she really had no idea what was going on. The visitation in December was considered the family's time to celebrate the holidays with a special dinner. Even in the worst parts of his addiction, I was always able to get Gerad in front of Tatum at home for Christmas, so we were anxious to have her attend. He put it off for as long as possible, but once I had bought her ticket to attend the visit at Burning Tree, he made the call. He said she was quiet, seeming not to know what to say or ask. His counselor sat with him during what he said was the most difficult call of his life. It was short and not as unpleasant as he'd feared. He told her he was excited to see her, and she said the same. On the flight down, she told me she had a friend whose dad was in rehab, so they had something in common. She was amazingly mature and accepting. Kids are remarkably resilient and can often find the silver lining in the darkest of clouds. Gerad's stepfather also flew down, and as we drove to The Ranch, she was animated and talkative.

As we pulled up, I could see Gerad through the window, hands in his pockets, shoulders pulled down, anxiously awaiting our arrival. He looked more apprehensive than usual, and I know he was unsure of his daughter's reaction. All that anxiety quickly disappeared as she ran to see him, opening her arms for a hug. She clung to him tightly and only left his side to check out the dogs and play with some of the other kids there to visit their parents. Before we left, he took her aside and asked her if she had any questions. She wanted to know if his addiction was why he hadn't shown up to some of her birthdays or school events. He answered her truthfully until she seemed to get all her thoughts out. Once she seemed satisfied with all the answers, she gave him a big hug and then ran off to say goodbye to the dogs and her new friends. I smiled, thinking she was just as good at making friends as her daddy.

Tatum came with me on several visits. We would arrive a day or two early to make a weekend out of it. We shopped at the "biggest mall ever," according to Tatum, attended a children's theater production, and went to Six Flags. She enjoyed staying in a hotel, eating out, and, most of all, going to The Ranch. It became an easy routine for her, and she never appeared ruffled or put out about what was happening. She adapted and enjoyed their short time together, and it lifted Gerad's spirit, finally giving him his "Why?"

The counseling updates were insightful, but they only shared what Gerad was comfortable sharing. Occasionally Keyana would ask about Gerad's history with his father, brothers, and daughter to clarify issues he brought up. She explained that Gerad was still having trouble holding people accountable, and he focused on helping people through their issues rather than dealing with his own. As he had been before his addiction, others were drawn to him, trusted him, and would confide in him. She explained the EMDR treatment he was going through. Gerad had never processed his accident and remembered very little about that day or his time in the hospital. The sessions carefully brought him back to that day, and he was able to remember and process what happened. It also brought up unpleasant memories of incidents with his father, but again, it allowed him to look at them from a different perspective and move forward.

From the beginning, Gerad's counselor let me know that Gerad had surrendered to treatment and was working hard to get through it. Many had not. Some people had been to rehab so many times they learned to say and do the right things to appear to be cooperating and working toward sobriety but never actually giving in emotionally, mentally, or spiritually. They were generally smart, successful, and manipulative. It had worked for them their whole life, and they resorted to what they knew. Although they flew through the program ahead of everyone else, none remained sober once they got out on their own.

When Gerad was first admitted to The Ranch, the counselors had asked about family involvement in his treatment plan. I became the main point of contact and had them ask Gerad if he wanted his dad to be part of the updates. I think he was hopeful his dad would want to be part of his recovery, so I agreed to contact him and let him know what was going on. I had very few interactions with my ex-husband in the years leading up to this time. He had moved to another state, and the extent of our contact was his sending a Christmas card to my address for the boys or a birthday present to Tatum. I texted him and let him know Gerad was in rehab and asked if he wanted to help. His reply was that he had no money. I assured him I wasn't asking for his help financially, but it was important he be part of Gerad's recovery, which meant nothing more than taking a call every other week from Gerad's counselor. He agreed. I let him know when visitations were, although he never attended one, but he did agree to attend the Family Program late in Gerad's time at The Ranch. It was a step all clients had to go through before moving on to Phase Two, which was getting weekends at the sober living house in Dallas. After several months of weekends, the client would graduate to Phase Three and move into the sober house for six months. It was a step everyone looked forward to, but there were several hurdles to get there, one of the hardest being the Family Program.

The commitment to the Family Program was a big one, not only emotionally but financially and timewise. They wanted select family members to come down for what would be nearly a week with travel time. Gerad's counselor felt it was critical that both of his brothers attend, along with his father and me. I told her I would talk to my boys, but she would have to get his father to attend. No one would tell you exactly what happened at Family Program, but when I asked the mothers I met during visitation how it had gone, I got anxious stares and comments like, "I don't want to go through that again," and "It was awful." I asked Gerad's counselor to be honest with my ex about what the program entailed and that it was not just another visitation. I let her know he hadn't experienced Gerad's spiral into addiction, not even realizing Gerad had lost the use of his arm until long after the fact. She explained that the program wasn't about the addiction but about the family dynamics that could sabotage recovery. She stressed again that his father would be an important part of that and assured me she had been clear about what he was getting into. He had still agreed to attend.

My oldest son didn't hesitate when asked to come, even though he knew his father would be there. They hadn't spoken in years. Gerad and Ryan were different in so many ways, and their lives had gone in such different directions, but Ryan always came through for him when it mattered. My youngest son wasn't quite as receptive. I waited to ask him until we were on a trip to Montana, checking out a college he wanted to attend. It was now or never, with the Family Program less than a month away. As we pulled up to our hotel on our last night, I asked him if he would consider taking the trip to Dallas. Before he could answer, I explained as much about it as I knew and let him know Ryan and I would be attending, as well as his father. His immediate reaction was, "No way." I spent the next 20 minutes telling him that it was important for Gerad and that maybe he would get the chance to say some things to his father that he had bottled up. Reluctantly, he finally agreed but let me know he wasn't happy about it. All my boys are so different and aren't especially close. Age and distance hadn't helped bridge that gap, but I was hoping this program might help heal us all.

July came about quickly, and Ryan, Alec and I left for Dallas to participate in the Family Program with four other families. We checked into our hotel outside of Dallas, closer to The Ranch, since we would be going back and forth over several days. Although it was held in the same building we used for regular visitation, the Family Program would be held upstairs in a large room rather than in the first-floor dining facility. We signed in and sat down in the dining facility to get an overview of the program. Gerad's dad was there first, and after greeting us, Gerad headed to his table. It had been a long time since any of us had seen their dad, and an awkward silence followed. Gerad seemed oblivious and chatted with him.

The Ranch's Clinical Director and a therapist from outside the facility would facilitate the program together. The Clinical Director had been through all the client's journeys and was familiar with their stories. The outside therapist was familiar with The Ranch but did not know the clients or their stories. Each client had a variety of family members with them; sisters, mothers, fathers, and brothers in various combinations. We moved upstairs and took our seats. Each client introduced the family that had come by, standing behind them as we sat in a circle. The introductions were followed by a brief statement about the family member. Gerad's introduction of his father was surprising and honest. He choked up as he introduced me. Each client also described their addictions. We were told we would remain in that room for the entire weekend and would be expected to follow the same rules as the clients: accountability, honesty, participation, and authenticity. There were several exercises we went through to open communication and several observances by the mediators. We were given homework; questions to answer about Gerad to bring to the next day's session.

Toward the end of the evening, the focus started with our family by the therapists asking Gerad a question about his relationship with his father. After several comments by Ryan and Alec, they were asked to come closer to their father as they spoke of hurt, loss, and disappointment. The exchanges got heated as emotions boiled to the surface. The therapists worked at getting their father's acknowledgment of the boys' feelings and keeping the dialogue constructive. It was painful and stressful for everyone, and began to feel like a confrontation with years of issues boiling to the surface. The audience of clients and their families oddly gave the boys a safety net to say what they had wanted to express most of their lives. It was explosive, and something neither the clients nor therapists would forget any time soon. Their father's reaction was subdued and stunned as he deflected the therapist's attempt to have him acknowledge their fractured relationship. As the time came to a close, their father and everyone else couldn't get out of there fast enough. Our family was asked to stay. There was a consensus that Gerad's dad would not come back for day two and that the boys would probably never get the apology they sought. We drove back to the hotel to complete our homework. I was exhausted, but Ryan and Alec spent hours sitting outside talking. Boxed-up memories of hurt and disappointment flooded back to all of us, and we were anxious about day two.

To the surprise of everyone, Gerad's dad showed up for day two. The therapist's first question was, "How many people thought that Gerad's dad wouldn't show up today?" Everyone raised their hand, including him. It provided a moment of levity to start the day. Our homework had been a series of questions to go over one-on-one with Gerad. His father and I went first, and the boys did theirs together as we looked on. We were asked about our emotions as we heard the exchanges. At the beginning of the program, they explained that there are five basic emotions, and when asked what we were feeling at that moment, we were to respond with one of them. There were several mentions of my father by the boys. He had been a larger-than-life presence in their lives, and we all missed him terribly. Listening to their comments, I was struck by how desperately they had been looking for a father figure and how he had filled that gap. He died too soon, and it left a giant void. I got

175

choked up as I realized how we had failed the boys. There were no takebacks, only the emotional wreckage of a marriage that should never have happened and lasted too long. The boys bore the brunt of our mistakes.

Thursday was a very long day for all of us, but there were some important moments. Gerad's dad chose to participate more and contributed some important insight, but we were exhausted mentally and emotionally. They held a dinner for all of us downstairs. I wanted the boys to spend some time alone with their dad, but Alec insisted I join them. It was never comfortable, but I had let go of my anger toward him a long time ago. I sat quietly and allowed them to interact. Gerad and Alec kept the conversation flowing with their dad, but Ryan remained quiet. He abruptly left the table early and went outside. I went to look for him later and found him walking up and down the road. He was angry at Gerad for continuing to engage with his father. Ryan was nowhere near being able to forgive his dad, and he couldn't understand how Gerad could. I encouraged him to talk to Gerad about it so we didn't lose sight of the purpose of this program, which was honesty, accountability, and communication. I also encouraged him to take his father aside and talk to him as well. We went back inside, gathered our things, and said our goodbyes to Gerad. Once in the car, Ryan let loose about his feelings after Alec commented that all-in-all, it had been a pretty good day. Most of his anger was directed at me. He wanted to know if I would have left their father if I had known everything that was going on. I assured him I would have and asked why they felt they couldn't tell me. He wanted to know why Gerad was acting as though nothing had happened, and I tried to explain that Gerad had the advantage of nearly a year of therapy to gain perspective and come to peace with things that had happened. Each of them was an adult and could have a relationship with their dad where they created boundaries. It was a heated exchange at times, with raised voices and exasperation from all of us. We finally headed back to the hotel, where again Alec and Ryan stayed up to talk.

As we sat in the car to head back to The Ranch for day three, Ryan said he was going to take his dad aside at breakfast. He wanted to tell him he didn't know if he could ever forgive him but wanted to see if there was a way forward. When we walked in, he headed straight to his dad and asked him to join him outside. Ryan looked calm; his dad looked terrified. Whatever was said, they returned to breakfast composed and quiet. Baby steps.

What we looked forward to the most on day three was getting to take Gerad off The Ranch for the afternoon and evening. He wanted to go to dinner and a movie that wasn't rated G or PG, the only kind allowed at The Ranch. It was the first time we had all been together in ten years. Alec had to go back that evening so he could go to work on Monday, so I took him to the airport while his dad and brothers returned to the hotel. Alec and his dad agreed to talk every Sunday. He left on a high note. Ryan and his dad also agreed to stay in contact, and the goodbyes between the boys were heartfelt. I hoped that it was a start toward healing.

Chapter Ten

Transformation: Gerad

"It's hard to forget pain,
But it's even harder to remember sweetness.
We have no scar to show for happiness.
We learn so little from peace."
Chuck Palahniuk

The next year of treatment became routine. Waking up at 6 am to pray and meditate with a group of guys, do chores for an hour and a half, group until 4 pm, and have an outside meeting somewhere in Dallas. I forgot what it was like to live a consistent life, and it was much more fulfilling than the chaotic wreckage I left behind. I knew what to expect on each day of the week and relearned life skills that I took for granted. We would cook and clean as a community, and I gained a lot of self-esteem from doing things for myself and the others around me. When you spend that much time in treatment with a group of people, you naturally become close to everyone. I learned all their deepest darkest secrets, and they knew mine. It was a place to be vulnerable with a little poking and prodding from the staff. I needed to be pushed to come out of my shell. My natural state was to sit back and observe the room. It was a survival technique that I had used my whole life. I was constantly walking on eggshells and scanning for danger. This place was built for addicts like me. No one slipped through the cracks here, believe me, I tried. They put the spotlight on me a lot, and it was super uncomfortable.

I came into treatment with the attitude that drugs were the problem and there was nothing else to work on. I later came to understand that drugs were my solution for the pain and the trauma that I experienced in my life. They worked for a long time but, at some point, stopped being viable and left a path of destruction. Burning Tree and another program helped me unearth the real issues. There were two big things identified that I had never dealt with: my motorcycle accident and the tumultuous relationship with my dad. It was uncomfortable to talk about those things because I wanted everyone to validate my feelings and feel sorry for me. One of the best pieces of advice I got was from another client. He told me several times, "Victims don't stay sober."

The first thing I worked on was my motorcycle accident. I decided to move forward with Eye Movement Desensitization and Reprocessing (EMDR) therapy. This was an interesting experience and was difficult to go through, but I wanted closure on my motorcycle accident. I would relive the moments with a counselor and take note of my thoughts and beliefs about myself at the time of the accident and what I believed then. My right arm never got full function back, and I spent so much time trying to hide it from others. Most people that meet me don't even notice it, but I do. This is how I view trauma for everyone. We only see what's on the surface, or maybe even the tip of an iceberg that has so much mass beneath. You never know what people are dealing with, and we keep conversations surface-level. "Hey, how are you?" "Fine." I had to explore the idea of feeling less than everyone else to make any headway. I avoided talking about it since it happened. I still avoid it today. Like anyone with a disability, I want to be treated as an equal. I also needed to recognize my limitations and ask for help when necessary. I will never be able to do pushups or pull-ups or lift anything heavy above my head, but I can focus on my strong attributes and find my worth in this world. We would always talk about mantras during our sessions. The one that stuck out to me and that I still use today is, "I am more than my arm. That's not what defines me." I did EMDR sessions for seven months while I was an inpatient. It helped me come to terms with who I was and who I didn't want to be. Another eye-opener was seeing the beliefs that I had about myself were there long before my accident. Things like "I'm not good enough," "No one will ever love me," and "I'm ugly." I made myself feel less than from day one, and it was comforting to know that these beliefs and the pain that I had didn't come down to one single moment in my life. I built my confidence back step by step and faced some ugly shit in my life. The only way to get better was to stop avoiding and go straight through the fire.

Then there was the issue of my dad. Things weren't always bad between us, or I guess a better term is estranged. When I was little, I saw my dad as a hero that was full of life and hard to hurt. He had this ability to get angry at something and then seemingly move on like nothing had happened. As I started to grow up, there were things that terrified me. He drank a lot and would come home late at times to divey out punishment. The moment that changed everything was also the same moment he poured beer into my mouth. This was the moment that changed our relationship forever. It didn't seem like a big deal at the time, but I became much more cautious around someone that I had viewed as a hero. The trust just wasn't there anymore. This was also the same time that he would go on long trips to recruit football players. I started to dread when he would come home, and I was afraid of what his next move might be. EMDR helped me acknowledge experiences like that and relate them to how they would show up in my current life. I was a master at avoiding conflict and was always hyper-aware of my surroundings and the people in them.

Family Program was a well-kept secret at The Ranch. Nobody would tell you what took place, and I built up a lot of anxiety as it approached. It was confirmed that my whole family would be attending, including my dad. This was the first time we were all together in the same room in over ten years. I played so many different scenarios in my head as the day got closer. I was hoping that everyone would get some closure and much-needed healing.

I prepared to face my dad in the weeks leading up to seeing him. I worked closely with my counselors on how to approach him properly and voice my experience appropriately. I spent most of my life always wanting answers from him or needing him to admit the terrible shit that he had done. I told myself, "If only he acknowledged what had happened, I would feel better," but I found out how false that narrative was. He was this big monster in my head for so long, and I gave him a lot of power over me. His words were sharp and could cut right through my soul. He had the ability to make me cry in a few short sentences, and I hated it. I became a victim of him, and I was trapped with no way out. The therapy and other programs helped me come to terms with the reality around him. I was able to forgive him by taking a deep dive into my relationships and looking at the facts of what happened. I found mistakes I had made and saw this wasn't a one-sided battle. I knew the things he did to my brothers and me weren't right, but God gave me the ability to forgive him for my own peace.

Getting sober was the hardest thing next to heroin addiction because the change didn't happen overnight. I was used to instant gratification or a quick fix. Recovery is a slow and steady process, and I couldn't see the change in myself until I saw my dad in that setting. I remember the feeling so clearly. There was a point where my brothers were venting their frustrations toward my dad and wanting him to apologize and answer for his past digressions. We were all sitting in a circle facing each other with five other families in the room. As the tension in the room rose, I could see people getting uncomfortable and starting to squirm. My little brother was turning beet red as his voice escalated, and I could see the pain in his eyes from all the unanswered questions and gaps we were trying to fill in. He was far more emotional than my older brother, who was blunt and brutally honest with him. My dad reacted like he always did in these interactions and denied everything that was being said. What was interesting for me was the way I stayed calm while the melee was happening in front of me. It felt like there was a bubble around me in that room, and I thought, "Holy shit, I'm not reacting like I normally would." When it was my turn to say my piece, I handled it calmly and objectively. I told him about the time that he poured beer into my mouth and how I felt fear and pain. For the first time, it didn't matter if he acknowledged me or not. I found that when I framed it in a manner that wasn't accusatory or offensive, I got a far better response than I expected. He looked human to me for the first time in recent memory, and I felt relief that the "Monster" wasn't there anymore. The first day of the program was volatile, and everyone expected my dad not to come back. I was walking with him after the first day was over and his eyes were locked on the exit. He was the first one out the door, and his pace suggested that he was never looking back. I softly asked, "See you tomorrow?" He answered without breaking stride, "I'll be back. See you tomorrow."

The more that I addressed issues from my past, the more I realized that drugs were an escape from all the underlying issues. Drugs were a great life raft and a powerful solution for a while until they stopped working, and the consequences far outweighed the benefits. I came into sobriety with the belief that heroin and meth were my problems, but really it was a Band-Aid for all the pain and suffering that I felt inside. The Family Program emphasized that addiction was a "family disease," and it made more sense to me as everything unfolded.

The first step in my getting sober was my mom cutting me off entirely. She enabled my behavior for a long time, and I often wondered how hard it would be to cut off your child. She mentioned that it was the hardest thing she ever did, and I didn't make it easy on her. Helping an addict goes against every parental instinct. My mom naturally wanted to help solve my issues for me, but it would have killed me if she had kept giving me money and a place to stay. I had to want it for myself before anything changed.

The counselors recommended an outside program for all family members to attend and gave them the resources to find help in their hometowns. Powerlessness affects everyone; and wanting to control an addict's behavior can be deadly. We all learned about the different roles each family member played and where the dynamics were failing or unhealthy. It was cathartic to talk about the pain and anger, but also relieving to hear the love that we all had for each other. Communication falls into the shadows in a family, and it's tragic. A lot of the frustrations and fear in my family were swept under the rug around my using, and it was helpful to talk about it in a group setting.

The best part was being able to hang out with my family off the property. It felt like we went through a war together and came out triumphant. There was laughter and joy in the air, and everyone looked peaceful. It was a symbol of love and remembrance of a time before everything got so complicated. Ryan and I accompanied our dad to his hotel. We sat in the lobby for a couple of hours, talking and catching up on everything. It was nice to be present and engage with them. It was exciting to see my older brother and dad talking about life, and I had hope for their relationship moving forward. Dad took me back to The Ranch, and I felt so much gratitude for the way things had happened up to this point. Maybe things were finally going to be different in my life. My perspective had shifted.

Chapter Eleven

Letting Go: Lisa

"Looking back, it's funny what you learn in life.
You learn how to feel and how to love.
You learn how to outlast pain
when it's something you believe in and
sooner or later, you learn how to let go."
Jonathon Muncy Storm

Soon after Family Program, Gerad graduated to weekends spent at the sober house in Dallas, bringing him one step closer to leaving The Ranch. He had been looking forward to this moment for a long time, having watched friends progress to this stage before him. The clinical team would decide when he was ready to reside there full-time, beginning the aftercare portion of the program.

The Burning Tree program spans three years if you complete all the recommended phases. Phase One is an inpatient at The Ranch, Two is the sober living house, and Phase Three is moving, preferably with someone else from the sober living house, to an apartment or house in the Dallas area. In Phase Three, continuing to rely on the support system you have built, attending meetings, and being of service to others are considered critical to your success. You only have to complete the first two phases to attend graduation, but most that get that far have received significant encouragement, including a home 12-Step group, friends they made at The Ranch, and are actively sponsoring others in the beginning stages of recovery.

In preparation for his permanent move off The Ranch, Gerad would need to open a bank account and get a Texas driver's license. Such mundane things before were now milestones. He would be entering the real world again, and that would require transportation. Ryan had agreed to drive Gerad's truck to Texas to coincide with one of the scheduled visitations so he and I could fly back together. Ryan didn't hesitate to volunteer, despite the fact the truck was far from a luxury ride and the long distance from Nevada to Texas.

As he moved into Phase Two, Gerad was responsible for finding transportation, not only for the future but to and from the sober house for his weekend trial. It was an important step in his progress to regaining trust and accountability. And there's the fact that you can't exactly call a cab to get back into Dallas from The Ranch. That truck was a connection to Gerad's old life, so I spent hours scouring it for needles, drugs, and other paraphernalia prior to Ryan's road trip. Gerad told me in one of our weekly calls that he had checked the truck for any drugs prior to our trip to admit him into Burning Tree in a desperate attempt at one final high. Even after four months in jail, which meant four months sober, two felony charges he had a chance to erase, and facing the best chance he had ever had to get sober, the pull to use and check out remained strong. Because I was watching him like a hawk to make sure he arrived sober, he said he had been rushed searching his truck so I wouldn't catch him, which left a chance that something was still there. Despite my best efforts, the inspection of the truck at Burning Tree turned up a few items I missed. I had not mastered the art of thinking like an addict the way they had. It takes an addict to know an addict.

October 2019 marked a new beginning in Gerad's journey. He moved into his room at the men's sober house, leaving The Ranch and officially entering stage two of the program. It was both a celebration and a concern. New freedoms brought with them opportunities to make mistakes. At The Ranch, every moment was occupied, and all precautions were taken. Monitoring was easier in this closed environment. Failure at The Ranch only came about by leaving The

Ranch. As long as you were there, you had a chance to work things out. In the aftercare program, each client had to take the tools they had learned and apply them in the real world. The only way to know if you could apply those lessons is to get back out there. Although I was excited and hopeful for Gerad, I slept a whole lot better when he was at The Ranch. When your hopes have been dashed so many times, you are afraid to be hopeful. I couldn't imagine when that feeling would change. It was like waiting to exhale.

In aftercare, he was required to find a job, set a budget, and meet weekly with the Aftercare Director. He would continue to see a therapist as well. Although I paid for his first month's rent, he was expected to cover all his expenses going forward. It had been a long time since that had happened. Everyone had to follow the rules, including continuing to hold each other accountable. They could be drug tested at any time during their stay. The goal was to give them the skill set to move out on their own after six months. The first few weeks were an adjustment period for Gerad as he got used to some of the freedoms he had been without for more than a year, most importantly, time that wasn't scheduled. Learning how to use downtime constructively was a skill he needed to learn. He mentioned on one of our early phone calls that he kept feeling like he was "doing something wrong when he wasn't busy." He seemed to adjust quickly and began enjoying outings to celebrate birthdays and sober anniversaries with fellow alumni. I loved seeing the social media posts of the beaming group out and about around Dallas.

I remember him telling me, during one of his sober periods, that it was strange to be idle. Whenever he was trying to get sober, he would spend the first week sleeping. It was the kind of exhaustion that only those that don't know where they will sleep at night can know. On the streets, he moved from morning to night, looking for a fix, looking for the money to pay for a fix, looking for a place to stay or at least a place to sleep. You left the place you were sleeping at dawn to avoid getting roused by an annoyed business owner or the police and didn't settle into a new one until well after most of the city was asleep. During the day, he hunted down people that owed him something and kept moving to avoid those he owed. It required him to constantly keep moving. He went from hustling on the streets to jail and The Ranch, where every moment was scheduled. "Idle hands do the devil's work," as my grandmother used to say. We had always tried to fill his days during his previous attempts to get sober, if only it was that simple. I was happy for him now that he got to appreciate what most of us take for granted.

The Aftercare Director gave me the same assessment of Gerad that the counselor at The Ranch had given me; Gerad was ready to make this change. Maintaining a schedule remains important in all stages of recovery. Aftercare was the cautionary stage, as those newfound freedoms often came with bad choices. Some people wouldn't follow the rules of the house and had to leave, some chose not to participate in aftercare at all, and several relapsed once they moved out on their own. Once again, I cheered their successes and mourned their failures. I had learned some of their stories intimately at Family Program, and those relapses are the ones I mourned the most. As I learned, relapses often become part of the recovery process, but it still stung every time Gerad mentioned one. It was my own fear and insecurities about Gerad that always bubbled to the surface. Although Gerad lost contact with several people, and several stayed in contact even though they were no longer sober, those that remained in the area often got back into a program and tried again. Hearing about their struggles always caused anxiety, but Gerad continued to assure me that he didn't think about using anymore. I smiled when he posted pictures of large groups of friends celebrating, well, anything and everything, freedom mostly. Dallas offered many things to do, and I was happy to see him take advantage of them. As much as I wanted to be hopeful that he would get his life back, it also felt like an abrupt adjustment from years on the addiction merry-go-round. Dare I hope?

I could only vaguely remember what life had been like before all this happened, or maybe I was just afraid to let my mind go off high alert and step back, allowing him to take the lead and find his way back. I wasn't sure I knew how to let go, but I knew it was no longer my place to guide him; this was his journey, and I had to accept that it was his decision to find success or failure. I had to stick by my promise to him when Alec and I attended his post-admit intervention. I had given him the best chance at recovery, but the rest was up to him. If he failed, he would no longer be able to participate as part of this family. I would have to let him go. Doubt crept in as I wasn't sure I knew how to do it.

He got a job, attended meetings, and volunteered to tell his story to those just starting their recovery. It had proven challenging for him since participating meant telling his story to groups of people he didn't know. His first time, he called the Aftercare Director from the parking lot for a boost of confidence. He was nervous about the reactions to his story. He was pleasantly surprised at their acceptance, and it helped assuage his insecurities. He quickly went on to sponsor several men at a time, including some from The Ranch.

This was also the time all the clients would schedule time home to work on their amends. A friend in recovery is required to accompany them, and the trip is limited to a few days. He had made several very close friends when at The Ranch, and he chose Gabe to accompany him. They were close in age, had been roommates, and hit it off immediately upon Gerad's arrival at The Ranch. Their stories had a lot in common. Gerad chose his stepfather, grandmother, brothers, and me to start the amends process. Many of the things were hard to hear and opened old wounds further as we realized we only knew a small portion of the lies and deceit. Still, everyone was grateful for the honesty and apologies and saw it as a way to move forward. Amends are a big part of the recovery process, and Gerad would continue for the next year, completing his list. It is strange, but everyone's reaction was similar, discomfort. "It wasn't so bad," "I didn't mind," "It was my fault too." We went right back into the pattern of excusing his behavior. My mother just kept talking over him, avoiding acknowledging all his apologies. Clearly, we all had more to learn.

Then the COVID-19 pandemic hit. The nationwide shutdown would prove particularly hard on those in recovery. The Aftercare Director required that each client give her a daily schedule once most of their workplaces shut down, including Gerad's. He began running, but the isolation of Zoom-only 12-Step meetings, no work, and no dinners out with friends took its toll. He couldn't travel home and looked forward to finding an apartment and getting out of the house where he now spent most of his time. Texas opened up sooner than most, and he was able to get back to work in weeks rather than months, like much of the country, but he did take a financial hit. The subsidies from unemployment helped once he was able to qualify. He found a roommate from the sober house, and together they found an apartment in an area where other clients now lived. As with most addicts, Gerad had ruined his credit, but his scores began to climb during his time in rehab. I guess no credit activity happening is seen as a step in the right direction. He had spent years signing up for cell phones he knew he couldn't pay for, scouring the internet for loans with ridiculously high interest rates, and taking out credit cards until they wouldn't give them to him anymore. He had medical bills he never intended to pay and never made a single payment on those loans. In my misguided hope that things would turn around, I had continued to pay off the debts I found out about, hoping to give him a chance when he got sober. Addiction and jail have similar effects; both make it very hard to start over when you are ready. The drug-related arrests and misdemeanor theft remained for anyone to find in a background check, so I co-signed his lease and crossed my fingers. It felt like the biggest step to getting his life back, but we still had one more hurdle; he had to face the judges in Elko to receive his sentence on his drug felonies. After getting this far, we couldn't ignore that all this progress could end in one life-changing decision.

Court dates were finally set for the sentencing that had been postponed for Gerad to attend treatment. We were uncertain how much of a longshot it was to have his felonies dropped since Elko County did not have a drug court that promised to wipe your record clean if you were able to stay sober for a year. Gerad made arrangements to continue his amends when we were in Elko for court. It seemed like a hopeful thing to do since we were not sure of the outcome. We all breathed a sigh of relief when our attorney was able to get an agreement from the prosecutor and one of the judges to drop the charges without a court appearance.

As we entered the second judge's courtroom, it was evident he was in a foul mood. He grumbled about too much paperwork as he tried to sift through all the reports from The Ranch. Our attorney had to remind him of our proposal and request a dismissal of changes. The judge turned to ask Gerad questions as we held our breath. Finally, he said the words we had been waiting to hear and wished Gerad luck. Gerad was given probation to be transferred to Texas until all the paperwork went through. Our attorney turned around and grinned. My impulse was to run out of that courthouse as fast as possible. I was still used to the rug being pulled out again and again on this journey and still couldn't wrap my brain around being given a win. We stopped at the probation office on our way out of town and left Elko, never turning back as we disappeared down the highway.

I still received calls from the Aftercare Director as Gerad moved toward qualifying for graduation. Gerad had been seeing a therapist during his time at the sober house and chose to continue to see her after he moved to his apartment to "check in" and "stay focused." Ironically, he was seeing the therapist that had been part of the Family Program at The Ranch, so she now knew his story well. By all accounts, Gerad thrived at his job under a boss he truly liked working with and was able to steer others he knew to jobs at the same place. He had an excellent support system, even as those around him relapsed. He struggled with whether to come back to Reno to be near his daughter but begrudgingly realized the support system he built was important to maintain. If he didn't stay sober, coming to Reno would be meaningless, so he visited as often as he could and struggled with his right to be in Tatum's life, finally scheduling regular Facetime calls with her to develop a routine.

I felt it was important for Gerad to have a ceremony to mark his accomplishment of completing the program. Covid had other ideas. A graduation date would be set, then canceled and reset. Finally, a date was set in January 2021 with Covid restrictions firmly in place. Since vaccines were still not widely available, everyone in attendance had to have a negative Covid test. In addition, they limited the number of family members and guests Gerad could invite. It wouldn't be what I had first witnessed upon Gerad's admission, but it was still a graduation. Gerad's daughter, his older brother and I headed to Dallas. He wouldn't have a large audience of his peers or even all the staff that had been a part of his recovery, but he chose two good friends, and as luck would have it, his counselor, who had taken another job at the very end of Gerad's time at The Ranch, had returned to witness his triumph.

Gerad had taken the day off and picked us up from the airport. He took us to his workplace and introduced us; then we stopped for lunch at a place nearby that he often frequented. We were all in high spirits, talkative and animated. COVID-19 was still a factor, and the restaurant was less crowded than we expected. The staff was attentive and happy to have customers, many of whom they seemed familiar with as they joked and laughed. We took the now-familiar road to The Ranch, and I realized this would probably be my last trip there. It was a good way to end the many journeys there, and I felt fortunate the last trip was for graduation and not failure.

The graduation had been scheduled to coincide with another Family Program. It hadn't dawned on me that graduation is always scheduled during Family Program until the moment we pulled up and I saw the number of people. I guess they did it to give families in the middle of it all hope, as it did for me. Unfortunately, those in attendance were not those that knew the graduate, as it had been when I attended my first graduation, but they were people that could appreciate what a huge accomplishment Gerad had just completed. As we entered the building where the graduation would take place, I saw the same looks on the families' faces we had after the longest day of the Family Program, shell shock. As they filed in and found their seats at the long tables, exhaustion and a mix of every imaginable emotion was evident in the droop of their shoulders, the tear-stained cheeks, and the shuffling gate. They were a mix of anxious parents, bewildered spouses, and a smattering of brothers, sisters, uncles, and grandparents, all willing to be put through the emotional wringer to give their loved one, their family, a fighting chance.

We were warmly greeted, albeit masked and minus hugs, by the staff that would speak for Gerad, as well as the two alumni he had chosen to attend. It was good to see everyone in happier circumstances. Even the dogs running around The Ranch seemed more animated, sensing this was a joyous occasion. After a quick dinner and with everyone back in their seats, the clinical director welcomed us and briefly explained to the audience what was going on. I was asked to speak first. It was surreal to be standing at the podium, looking out at so many expectant faces instead of being one of them. I immediately thought of all the people that told me to give up on Gerad, and especially the therapist that told me I had to prepare myself that the most likely outcome was that Gerad would die. I called her before I left for this trip to let her know Gerad was graduating. Although I could only leave a message, the feeling was priceless.

The room was brightly lit, and I could see my reflection in the windows behind the audience as I stepped behind the podium. It was like being in a dream and watching this unfold as an audience member rather than a participant. I had written some notes to gather my thoughts but couldn't remember them. I thought about what I would have wanted to hear when I was in the seats they sat in now, so I spoke of my desperation to save Gerad and the fallacy I had come to believe that my love and determination alone would be enough. I spoke of the frustration of trying to get through to Gerad, that he was worth fighting for and that I would never give up, that life was worth fighting for, always. I read the lyrics of a song I thought perfectly described that mix of delusion, love, and unwavering devotion. The song is "Rescue" by Lauren Daigle:

You are not hidden, there's never been a moment
you were forgotten,
You are not hopeless, though you have been broken, your
innocence stolen,
I hear you whisper underneath your breath, I hear
your SOS, your SOS.
I will send out an army to find you
in the middle of the darkest night,
It's true I will rescue you.
I will never stop marching to reach you
in the middle of the hardest
fight. It's true I will rescue you.
There is no distance that cannot be covered over and over,
you're not defenseless, I'll be your shelter I'll be your armor.

Stubborn determination kept my blinders on, and this song became my anthem. I told them I was certain the song had been written by the mother of an addict, so I researched the artist and the song. Turns out the song was written about God's love and devotion to rescue those in pain. I remember thinking, "Huh." It never dawned on me it could be about anything else. Gerad's addiction had become woven into my everyday life. That discovery further emphasized the illusion I was under that I could rescue him. I confessed that it turned out it was Gerad's work, not mine, and Gerad's willingness to give into something bigger than himself that would move him past the addiction. It was the accountability to himself and others taught and expected at Burning Tree that put him on the path to recovery. It was Gerad's choice, not mine, and I could only give him the support to be able to make that choice. I wanted him to know how proud I was of him and that I was in awe of how far he had come. "I love you, Gerad," were my last words before I walked toward my seat and received a warm, tight hug from him. It was finally sinking in.

Ryan spoke next and focused his remarks on the audience before him. He wanted them to know that if Gerad could do it, so could their loved one. He emphasized that it would be extremely hard, probably the hardest thing they ever did, but to never give up hope. He was inspiring, and it perked up the audience and the staff.

Tatum brought down the house. I didn't expect her to speak, but she bravely strode to the podium and introduced herself. None of us knew what to expect, especially since she had said very little about the effect her dad's addiction had on her. She didn't hold back, describing how scary the last few years had been and her sadness at how much she had missed with her dad. She sobbed as she expressed her feelings, and the entire room was mesmerized. It was the first time I saw the audience really engage. The staff's eyes filled with tears, and Gerad sat stunned. It was difficult to watch, but in just a few minutes, Tatum had managed to illustrate the debilitating effect of addiction on its youngest victims. She spoke straight from the heart. It was a tough act to follow, and Gerad's two friends who spoke after her were still visibly shaken by what she had said. They recounted funny stories during their time with Gerad at The Ranch and described how much Gerad's friendship meant to them. It was a touching finish to the evening.

It was a magical, emotional rollercoaster of a night, and I reflected on how the last two-and-a-half years had come and gone in the blink of an eye. In just three months, Gerad would have his three-year sober anniversary. He still had a long road ahead of him, but I was finally able to move past hope into acceptance of where Gerad was in his journey, and it was his journey, no longer mine. I smiled and exhaled in relief. It felt good to hand it over to him and let the burden go.

Chapter Eleven

Letting Go: Gerad

"I'm proud of me because
I've survived the days
I thought I couldn't."
Charles Okocha

My time at The Ranch was coming to an end. The last week there was emotionally charged in many ways. It was bittersweet to make it through a year-long inpatient program, and I was nervous and excited about the new chapter ahead. My dad had a heart attack and had a quadruple bypass surgery that was successful. My reaction to that news shocked me when I burst into tears. I had so much hate in my heart toward him for much of my life. I knew that something had changed because I felt regret and pain that he was going through something like that, and the staff arranged a phone call so I could talk to him and wish him well. After feeling numb for so many years, it was strange to experience emotions on all levels, and it made me grateful for the time I had spent in treatment. A lot of what I got to do was sit through difficult, uncomfortable feelings and realize that they are as temporary as clouds in the sky. It was clear to me that I was stronger than I was when I arrived and had learned some great tools to deal with whatever lay ahead on the horizon. I was ready to take on the aftercare portion of the program.

The men's sober house was in Richardson, Texas, just north of Dallas. When I was in Phase Two, I was allowed to come and stay on the weekend to get acclimated to the new surroundings. These passes were a treat but also extremely stressful. I had to schedule my time and what I was doing down to the hour and turn it in to be approved by the staff. There was also a budget to keep and logistics to figure out each week to ensure we would be busy and effective during the weekend. These passes could be pulled at any time during the week at The Ranch. You never knew if you would make it out or not. The upside was we got to watch as much TV as we wanted and eat ice cream until we felt sick. Sugar was limited at Burning Tree, so most guys, including myself, would go all out. It was a glimpse of having free range to do what you wanted without having constant oversight and accountability. It became clearer why the transition was set up this way. I was going from an extremely structured environment to more of an open schedule.

When I officially moved into the house, there were moments of anxiety and doubt. I felt like I was doing something wrong, and it took me a while to settle into the new surroundings. Everyone was required to get a job shortly after moving in, and I was lucky enough to find one within the first week, working at a consignment store. Aftercare really showed me the stark reality of addiction, and I began seeing how difficult it was for people with this disease to adjust to real life. When you're in treatment with people for a year, you expect everyone to make it, and when they go back out, it hurts. I got to see powerlessness from a different point of view, the one my mom had for so many years, watching me kill myself and selfishly destroy all my relationships. The sad fact is that you become jaded to people relapsing and even dying because it's so common. I needed to put what I had learned over the previous year into practice. As an addict, I don't like being uncomfortable. Doing things like meeting new people or joining a home group in a 12-step program went against my logical sober mind. My natural state is to retreat from everything and isolate. This is where aftercare was beneficial. I was pushed out of my comfort zone constantly and was encouraged to seek connection with others. I learned what worked for other people and got to see firsthand what didn't. It's a steep learning curve learning how to live life sober after using for so many years. I believed that life would be easier without drugs, but life is hard for everyone. The time in the house gave me the space and guidance to deal with issues in a healthy way, tackling problems head-on instead of avoiding them and hoping they would just disappear on their own. An issue that was on my mind a lot was my sentencing. The time had finally arrived to face the consequences of my actions and I was so terrified of the outcome. I headed to Reno with a close friend on a mission to do a couple of things. Learn what my actions had earned me and start making amends to those I had harmed.

Smaller towns like Elko move at their own pace, and I was concerned about having to see both judges in one day. We left Reno around 4:30 am to make the four-hour drive to be there ahead of schedule. My plan was to track down as many people as possible that I had either stolen from or harmed to see what I could do to make it right. I was taught to fix the relationships from my past to the best of my ability.

When we arrived, we went straight to the courthouse to see how the schedule would play out. My lawyer was there and started talking to the clerks and the District Attorney to make sure everything would go smoothly. He was a family friend to us and completely unorganized when it came to paperwork, but he was a damn magician in the courtroom. His personality was perfect for winning people over and persuading the room to listen to his pleas. He managed to circumvent one of the judges and got my charges dismissed as soon as we arrived. I only had one judge to worry about now, and we all heard rumors that he was a hard ass when it came to sentencing. When we finally made it in the courtroom, my lawyer had the judge laughing almost instantly, and I felt a lot of hope as the tension left the room. I ended up with a deferred sentencing tentative on completing a year of probation. I couldn't have dreamed of a better outcome, especially since I had several felony charges for drugs. Most small towns throw the book at you for drug charges, so I was more than grateful. My mom and I were elated at the outcome and left the courthouse with our heads held high. I was proud of the work I had put in over the last two years, and the benefits were starting to show themselves.

My other mission was underway, and I started reaching out to the people I had harmed to see if I could meet up with them. The most memorable of these was an old sober house manager who I lied to about going to meetings and searching for work when I was really going to the library every day. I was also sending mail for a girl that was in treatment through the sober house mailbox since they weren't allowed to send mail out from the facility. He confronted me about it one day, and I lied to his face. I contacted him, and he was surprised. I remember him saying, "We didn't leave on bad terms, did we?" I told him, "No, I just need to apologize for some dishonesty and see what I can do to make it right." He sounded skeptical but said he would meet me at the treatment center when he was done eating lunch. This amends was powerful because he told me that I was obviously a changed person if I was going out of my way to apologize for something that he didn't even remember. "My only goal for everyone I see is to plant a seed that will grow into something beautiful," he said with tears in his eyes. I hugged him and told him how much I appreciated his guidance and patience. You never know what some kind words and appreciation will do for someone.

I left Elko that day feeling like I was doing things right for the first time in a long time. I got pulled over for speeding on the way back to Reno, and instantly my heart sank. My past experiences of getting pulled over had all ended with me in handcuffs and going to jail. I still get nervous every time I encounter the police. The officer approached my window and said, "Good afternoon, Sir." I thought to myself, "Sir? Who the hell is he talking to?" This moment was important because I finally saw the change in myself that I had been looking for during the last two years. It was obvious that I was a changed man just by how the cop treated me that day. He left me with a warning, which had also never happened to me before, and told me to get home safe. The trip to Elko was a change in perspective. I felt useful and hopeful for the first time since my motorcycle accident.

Life felt different, and it was easier to flow with the water instead of trying to go against the current on my own self-propulsion. I was still in aftercare when Covid started, and I was able to adjust accordingly. I was laid off for a couple of months with a lot of time on my hands. I worried about idle times being sober, but it was obvious that I had a new set of skills to deal with life on life's terms. I began running for the first time in my life and set a goal to run five miles in under an hour. It took me about six weeks to accomplish, but most importantly, it gave me a goal and a sense of direction when so many things were uncertain at that time. I can't imagine how difficult it was for people who were trying to get sober when everything was shutting down.

Another cool experience was attending Zoom meetings with people from all over the world. I even got to share my experience with a group of people in New York. Addicts and alcoholics are resourceful when things get tough. I also started a meeting with a friend at a local homeless shelter. I was so terrified before the first one that I called my case manager and asked her, "What if I don't have anything good to say?" She laughed at me and replied, "Weren't you homeless at one time? I'm pretty sure you have the experience to help guys there." That meeting was a temporary fix at the time because there weren't many places allowing people to come in and talk to the residents. This is where I experienced the power of service. A lot of the guys there were straight off the street or jail, and 80 percent of them didn't listen to the things we were saying, but I felt God in that room every time I was there, and I continue to carry the message every Friday. Being able to guide someone from a place like that into a functioning member of society is better than any shot of dope.

It was bittersweet as I approached the end of aftercare. I was worried about what life would look like without counselors, therapists, and constant accountability, but the truth was I was able to build a group around me and a routine that looked exactly the same when the time came. I had plenty of people around me to continue to guide me and love me for the man that I had become. I was a hopeless heroin junkie that got the chance to recover and help the ones who continued to suffer. There was purpose and meaning.

My graduation ceremony was delayed about six months from the day I completed aftercare. It looked very different from the ones I had experienced while I was in treatment. I was only allowed to bring two guests other than my family to celebrate. My mom, older brother, and daughter all came to support this milestone with me. I was proud of myself for getting through this difficult process and sticking to a plan for once in my life. As we pulled up to the treatment center, there was a banner that said, "The journey begins here," and I felt grateful for the new beginning and another chance at life.

We all gathered in the dining hall, and I got to hear heartfelt accounts of my impact from friends, staff, and family. My mom spoke about the difficulties of not being able to help an addict, no matter how much you love them. The way to help goes against every natural instinct of a mother's love for her child. My brother spoke of the harsh realities of watching an addict suffer, and how he was put in situations he never thought he would be in.

Then there was Tatum. My daughter's speech was unexpected. I joked with her about speaking for me leading up to that night. She was eleven years old at the time, and I underestimated her bravery in spilling her heart out to the world. When the time came, she shot out of her chair like the building was on fire. It's hard to know the toll you take on others' lives until they have the chance to speak about it out loud. She burst into tears and recounted the nights that she was terrified if I was going to live or die and expressed her gratitude to have her dad back in her life. The room was frozen in time, and teary-eyed as we all looked on in amazement. This was a spiritual experience for me as I got to hear the pain and joy blow like a hurricane through that room. When she was done, my hand was glued to my face, and my jaw hurt from holding my mouth open. She gave me a big hug and told me she loved me. She was the last to go before it was my turn, and it was a hard act to follow. I had to control my tears and steady my voice. I don't remember what I said that night, but I remember thinking back to the first graduation I attended, sitting in the far back corner of the room, doubting if I would ever make it behind the podium.

It was surreal to be two-and-a-half years sober. I failed so many times trying to beat this thing, but it takes what it takes. I came away from that program with a new set of skills for living and my family back in my life. I had real friends around me that cared about me and were willing to help me at the drop of a hat. That's all I ever wanted.

Chapter Twelve

Freedom: Lisa

"Freedom is not worth having if it does not include
the freedom to make mistakes."
Mahatma Gandhi

If you are reading this, chances are someone close to you is an addict. Now that I'm on this side of the nightmare, I thought about what I would have wanted to hear four years ago when I was sitting where you are. What words of wisdom could someone have given me? What lessons can I now pass on?

My son and I had some harrowing experiences, and I look back and wonder how we made it through those years of setbacks, heartbreaks, and craziness. I made so many mistakes, and I am still working on forgiving myself. I was as close to broken as I ever will be in my life, and yet I couldn't give up, wouldn't give up. I was willing to do anything to save him without realizing my willingness, determination, and even my love left me open to manipulation and failure. The hard truth is that no one gets sober unless they want to. Not if you beg them or shame them. Not if you use reason, guilt them, or deploy tough love. They must come to their own realization.

Today our life feels strangely routine. All the things we took for granted have become daily miracles: a bouquet of flowers for Mother's Day, a call "just because," a first subway ride in New York City, and laughter in everyday conversations. It has been a long time since I could look forward to those routines and believe in possibilities again. Experiencing addiction creates a series of cracks in your belief system; what is just, who is valuable, what is important, and what no longer matters. It blows up what you know to be true and breaks you in places you didn't know could be broken. In that brokenness, you begin rearranging the pieces in a different order and realize that the experience changes you in ways you did not see coming.

As I write this, there are three million opioid addicts in the United States and millions more in various stages of recovery. In 2021, 100,000 people died of opioid overdoses, the highest number on record. There is still more funding for prevention than treatment, and not enough of either. The injustices, the inequity, and the biases of addiction stick with you, and you can't unlearn what you now know to be true. It can happen to anyone, anywhere, anytime, and getting people to care enough to change it is an uphill battle. More people die from overdose than auto accidents and gun violence combined. Still, the truth is there is very little sympathy for the victims. It is just too sordid and too unsavory for people to imagine it can happen to them. I was one of those people.

I was told not to expect Gerad to be the same person he was before his addiction when he got sober. It turned out to be true, not only for Gerad but for myself. After speaking at a family orientation at The Ranch, David Elliot asked me, "Who had the bigger transformation, you or Gerad?" The truth is, we have both been forever changed.

Chapter Twelve

Freedom: Gerad

"There can be no greater gift than that
of giving one's time and energy to help others without
expecting anything in return."
Nelson Mandela

I continue to help those in need because I know its importance to my own wellbeing. My hope for this book is that it reminds people that they are not alone and, at the very least, plant a seed that will sprout at some point and turn into a beautiful life. The sad reality is that many addicts and alcoholics will die before ever getting help. I hope my experience will speak to someone who is hopeless, desperate, and ready for a change. Even if it saves only one life, it is more than worth it. There is a way out.

There were so many wrong turns I made along the way, but my beliefs were by far the hardest to overcome. I thought I was unique and unsavable, that no one would be able to relate to me. I looked for the differences in everyone's story to justify why they couldn't help me. The constant separation of everyone and everything kept me in a lonely boat out in a stormy sea, hoping to randomly hit the shore and save myself. I wanted to figure it out. I thought I was weak and broken. It was hard to admit defeat and ask for help. No amount of rock bottoms or external consequences can convince an addict that they have a problem.

Life doesn't get easier because you get sober, but it does become surmountable. I am human, so I will still make mistakes, but the ability to face challenges and not run from tough emotions makes it all worthwhile. My perspective has changed to enjoy the things I took for granted. I am lucky to be alive and have the family that I do. I'm not always happy, but the serenity and the ability to accept life on life's terms is a stark contrast from where I crawled here from. I get to be present for Tatum, my mom, and my family, who sacrificed so much to keep me intact. I get to cook for Thanksgiving, decorate for Christmas, and help with the thousands of little projects my mom has around the house. I missed too many years and never realized how important these little moments with family are to me.

I work with new guys that have come from the depths of hell, and the battle is never-ending. Relapse is part of the journey, and I know I needed a few to show me how fragile life really is.

To the parents, children, and loved ones of an addict, it's not your fault. I promise that they love you no matter what happens or what they say. We become wild animals, backed into a corner, trying to claw our way out to safety. There will be dark and painful times, but don't give up. Support them from a safe distance, and don't get in the way of them crashing and burning. The idea of wanting a new life must come from them, not from you. Find support, pray for them, and be ready when the time comes.